Celebrating
THE
American Home

Celebrating THE

50

American Home

Great Houses from 50 American Architects

Joanne Kellar Bouknight

The Taunton Press

The Taunton Press
Inspiration for hands-on living®

The Taunton Press, Inc., 63 South Main Street, PO Box 5506, Newtown, CT 06470-5506
e-mail: tp@taunton.com

Editor: Peter Chapman
Interior design: David Bullen
Layout: David Bullen, Lori Wendin
Illustrator: Scott Bricher

LIBRARY OF CONGRESS CATALOGING-IN-PUBLICATION DATA
Bouknight, Joanne Kellar.
  Celebrating the American home : 50 great houses from 50 American architects / Joanne Kellar Bouknight.
    p. cm.
  ISBN 1-56158-761-3
  1. Architect-designed houses--United States. 2. Architecture--United States--20th century. 3. Architecture--United States--21st century. I. Title.
  NA7208.B67 2005
  728'.37'0973--dc22
                  2004030744

Printed in the United States of America
10 9 8 7 6 5 4 3 2 1

ACKNOWLEDGMENTS

Writing this book was an exercise first in commitment, then in abandonment. As I studied each house, I could see myself living in it, cooking in the farmhouse kitchen and calling the boys in to dinner. Then I'd up and move, maybe to Louisiana, where we'd cook in the outdoor fireplace and eat on the deck in the cool breezeway. From a cliff in Nova Scotia to the plains of West Texas, I got to know one extraordinary house after another. Each house is different, and each captured my imagination and admiration. That's why I'm leading off these acknowledgments with thanks to the homeowners, architects, builders, and craftspeople who made these 50 houses. Some came with vision, some came with skills, each came to the task with a gift for celebrating a singular house. Thanks, too, go to the photographers who have brought these houses to life in the pages of Taunton Books over the years.

Architects John Connell, Duo Dickinson, Jeremiah Eck, Richard Hayes, and Kerry Dietz deserve medals of valor for nailing down the 50 houses. Thanks to Richard for his discussion of the architect's role in good house design, and to John, Duo, and Jeremiah for their essays on what makes a house worth celebrating and their in-a-nutshell observations on why these 50 houses are so appealing.

Taunton Books deserves the credit for coming up with the idea, and, as Duo says, for transforming the genre of coffee-table house design book from style to substance. Many thanks to Jim Childs, Maria Taylor, Peter Chapman, Paula Schlosser, Carol Singer, Robyn Doyon-Aitken, Melissa Possick, and Kathleen Williams.

All of us give our deepest thanks to friends and families who by now understand what it takes to make a book happen.

Finally, John, Duo, Jeremiah, and I wholeheartedly dedicate this book to our editor Peter Chapman, who is both wordsmith and ringmaster. As John says, Peter is comfortable with crushing deadlines, endless edits, and irascible personalities (not ours, surely). He cuts to the chase when confronted by tangled writing (not ours, of course), and is adept at keeping the core qualities of a book in mind from start to finish. And when we claim to have other lives, he knows we don't really mean it and talks us into another wonderful Taunton book. It *is* about the house, thanks to Peter.

Contents

THE ARCHITECTS

What Makes a Great American Home?

Every year since 1992, over a million

new houses have been built in the United States. Since that time, The Taunton Press has published over 400 houses in a series of books written by designers, builders, and architects. That's a lot of square footage on glossy paper, but a mere fraction of the total houses built. Most of us would drive right by the houses that have gone up over the last dozen years—maybe even our own houses—but there is something about these Taunton houses worth not only a second glance but also a detailed study. The published houses are all over the map—literally—and they also range in looks, size, materials, and cost. Their sheer variety begs the question, what makes a great house? And the second question is, of course, what is there about these houses that can inspire our own designs?

WHEN DRIVING BY THIS HOUSE, it's impossible not to be intrigued by the break in the handsome stone wall and the enticing view through the house to a pond and fields beyond. Built in the 19th century, the house was reconfigured to add a modern sensibility to the traditional structure.

The 50 houses don't follow just one design formula.

BEING TUCKED UNDER THE EAVES is no comedown for a master bedroom when the site is this beautiful and the design is responsive. Collar ties allow the ceiling to follow the roofline, so the full gable end wall can be filled with windows. Built-in storage keeps the scale comfortable.

After a lot of discussion, Taunton writers and editors unraveled a thread of core qualities that makes these houses stand out. This chapter will go over each of these qualities, but here's the list in a nutshell. Each house has:

• a just-right response to site and context,

• a comfortable scale both inside and out,

• livability that accommodates everyday life and special occasions,

• a deep respect for craft,

• and a distinctiveness that transcends the ordinary.

With these five qualities determined, Taunton invited a group of architects to spend a couple of days sifting through those 400 houses to find the 50 that exemplified Taunton's best houses. There were rules: only one house per architect and the architects who judged couldn't throw their houses into the pot, no matter how well the houses fit the criteria. There was lively discussion and pithy commentary, such as "a surgical use of scale," "making a bungalow out of a sow's ear," and "a jewel box but not as expensive as a jewel box—maybe it's a lunch box!" But after much debate, there was consensus on the final 50. Just as those original 400 houses were a mixture of shapes and sizes, these 50 don't follow just one design formula. Each of these houses celebrates those five qualities in a way that just feels right. So now let's take a look at those five core qualities, always keeping in mind that there's no single way to design a great house.

A HOUSE CLAD with wood and stone is deemed to be in concert with nature, but this glass house is just as in tune with its surroundings. Wall-to-wall transparency allows unconstrained views from earth to sky.

Context: Connecting with the Site

Connecting with the site is critical to good design; in fact, it's hard to find *any* part of a house design that doesn't boil down to responding to context. Context includes the physical characteristics of the site, the social and physical fabric of the neighborhood or community, and land-use requirements such as setbacks and area restrictions. The physical site consists of topography, climate, and flora and fauna. The fabric of the neighborhood or community comprises scale, color, style, and rhythm—all elements that give a place character. For example, are all the houses set back from the street the same distance? Are roof slopes the same? Historical precedents add another layer of context, with vernacular materials and details providing a palette of options, if desired. Finally, land use regulations hold sway over where a house sits and how big it is.

THE OWNER OF THIS RANCH HOUSE in Washinton state grew up here, but never experienced the spectacular view until she added on—and up.

All these elements of the site inform the design, and it's up to the architect, owner, and builder to interpret the information. But that's what can make designing a great house so exhilarating—it's a unique response to a unique place, as evidenced in each one of these 50 houses.

It will come as no surprise that many of the owners and architects of these houses spent months, even years, getting to know their sites. Ralph Rapson, architect/owner of the glass cabin in Wisconsin shown on p. 7, camped on his 40-acre site for several years before hammering in stakes. Architect Cass Calder Smith and his clients visited their site many times, finally realizing that they always parked on one side of a majestic grove of oak trees, then walked under the canopy toward the sun. This informed the decision to position the house south of the trees, with the two major oaks framing the walkway to the house and space for parking kept north of the grove. The owner of the ranch redo in Washington state had lived in her house as a child, then with her mother's blessing, hired Drager Gould Architects to radically change the house. The architects reoriented the house towards the outdoors and gave the house a lake view it never had before.

Suburban and city dwellers have the same need to connect with their sites. Architect Hugh Newell Jacobsen wrapped a Florida house around a private courtyard with swimming pool and giant palms (photo facing page) to create a new context of an oasis in a hot, humid, not-so private community. A townhouse owner in Washington, D.C., lived 15 years in an end unit before he had the chance to buy the adjacent unit, which laid claim to a small rear garden. His only firm request of his architect Mark McInturff was that the new space provide views to the garden and allow for views from the older space, too. Those visual connections to the site give both new space and old a bright, witty style and luminous interior.

The particulars of a site shape a good house. For example, not every hillside presents the same set of challenges. When a client requested a single-level house on a hillside in Napa Valley, California, Eric Haesloop of Turnbull Griffin Haesloop scooped out a chunk of the treeless hillside to make a level field for a house with outbuildings. On a steep hillside in Santa Fe, architect Michael Bauer took inspiration from the Pueblo Indian tradition of building multiple, stepping-stone units and broke up the adobe house into wings that pinwheel down the hillside.

Certainly a waterside house does not have a blank slate to write on, but neither is it cast in stone. Which suits a coastal site better, a tall, lighthouse-shaped house or the hunkered down shape of a fishing shack? Of course, zoning regulations rightly have a say in mat-

IN A SUBURBAN FLORIDA COMMUNITY, privacy and serenity are created by girdling indoor spaces around a courtyard with swimming pool and tall palms; this view is from the master bedroom's balcony.

Scale applies at every level of a house's design.

WHEN THE FAMILY CABIN on this rocky Maine site burned down, the owners had just months to rebuild or they'd lose the right to build so close to the water. The new house, which follows the original footprint, looks completely at home.

ters of scale. This book showcases several coastal houses, each with a different take on scale and proportion, and all shaped in part by zoning. Stephen Blatt's design for a house smack dab on a rocky coast in Maine owes its comfortable, New England cabin proportions to a requirement that the house follow the footprint and envelope of the previous house, lost in a fire. A Martha's Vineyard cabin designed by Mark Hutker Associates was required to follow the footprint of the fishing shack that had been there, but raise the first floor 5 ft. to avoid flooding. To keep the house low, architect Phil Regan split up the volume into two, single-story hip-roof shapes, which make for airy interiors but a relatively modest scale outside.

THIS MARTHA'S VINEYARD
CABIN was designed to lie low
rather than loom over the
dunes by dividing the space
into two, hip-roofed volumes.

Scale: Fit and Proportion, Inside and Out

A house worth celebrating is not only a good neighbor but a comfort to its owners, and scale has a lot to do with both. Having a handle on scale means understanding how a house fits into a neighborhood or a landscape, how people fit into the house, and how details sit into the overall design. In other words, scale applies at every level of a house's design, whether viewed from the curb or from the couch.

Proportion is a critical aspect of scale and one that's too often overlooked. For example, when a family outgrows a house, the easy solution is to tack on more space, but a too-big addition can ruin the scale of a house. Some people shed houses the way a hermit crab sheds shells, moving up to a larger house each time the family grows. But a prime location allows a house with good bones to grow, if the addition is made with a sympathetic eye to the scale and proportion of the house.

KITCHEN, DINING, AND LIVING SPACES are not divided by walls, but the post-and-beam structure both defines space and adds a formal dimension to the great room.

LOWERED SOFFITS encircling this eating/living space not only give the room a definite edge but add complexity and intimacy.

Today's houses tend to be larger in scale than their ancestors not only outside the house but inside. Great rooms, or open plans that connect several spaces, make sense with busy families and more stuff to accommodate and share. This open space makes a skillful use of scale critical to how comfortable a house feels. A large house can be a comfortable scale if rooms are scaled to match the function, and if large rooms have differentiated spaces in them, such as niches and areas with lowered ceilings. A kitchen can handle a tall ceiling, if that's desired, as people stand and move around in it, whereas a dining room may be more comfortable if the ceiling isn't too high, or, if the ceiling is high, a substantial chandelier shapes the light over the table in an intimate way.

As architect Sarah Susanka shows in a Minneapolis house, a soffit at the edge of the room or over a built-in seat, can provide intimacy in a large room. This doesn't mean that for a room to be cozy it must have a low ceiling. On the contrary, a high ceiling can provide a sense of serenity, as seen in the lovely 20-ft. high screened porch that's the center of family life in a house in the New Hampshire forest, designed by Charles Warren (photo below).

Finally, the best-fitting details are designed with a nod to scale and proportion. Several of these 50 houses were inspired by the Shingle style, including Estes Twombly's Rhode Island house (bottom photo p. 14) and Michaela Mahady's Minnesota house (top photo p. 14). The Shingle style featured tall, slim windows clustered

ALTHOUGH THIS SCREENED PORCH is 20 ft. high, its proportion, color, and sylvan setting give it an intimate and serene ambience.

Livability banks on a mix of public and private spaces.

both inside and out makes it easy to enjoy a waterfront house in all kinds of weather.

in ribbons of three or five, and while individual windows in these new houses are actually larger than their ancestors, they follow the proper Shingle-style proportion and look right at home.

Livability: How a House Works and How It Plays

A house with a high degree of livability makes staying home on Friday night the best option. On the surface, livability is a subjective notion, considering that one family's open plan may be another's idea of bedlam, but everyone agrees that comfort is high on the list of necessities in a livable house. Comfort doesn't require luxury but it does require attention to spaces and adjacencies that make it easy for inhabitants to work, socialize, and rest. One key to making a livable house is to provide sheltered outdoor space where owners can take in the view in relative comfort. Architect Peter Bohlin tucked an intimate, wisteria-entwined terrace between the main house and a new space so to allow for a northerly view of sunlit fields and

A MODERN-DAY interpretation of the Shingle style, this well-proportioned Rhode Island house fits perfectly into the coastal landscape.

THIS WINDOW SEAT in a cottage in the woods is more than a cozy niche. Its bigger-than-life scale and windows on three sides give it a character and outlook that make it the most coveted space in the house.

pond without the discomfort of westerly winds. And, of course, a screened porch magnifies the livability quotient in any house, anywhere; a good many of these 50 houses bear witness to that fact.

Indoors, the livability factor banks on a comfortable mix of private and public spaces, with a natural progression from one to another. Duany Plater-Zyberk's design for a coastal Florida house weaves both public and private outdoor spaces among enclosed spaces to make a variety of experiences. Privacy is in the eye of the beholder, and the neighbor. Houses with close-by neighbors, such as Susanka's Minneapolis house, Duany Plater-Zyberk's island house, and the canalside houses of Jacobson and Glenn Irani, all have side walls that are largely opaque and openings that are obscured by shades, landscaping, or translucent glass. Privacy in the wild is a different matter. Rapson's glass house is open to sky and

THERE'S HARDLY A MORE VALUABLE SPOT in a house than a screened porch, which extends outdoor livability a few hours more each day and a few months more each year.

ADDING A FEW EXTRA FEET to the living room of a coastal Florida house multiplies the utility and quality of the space. The bump-out has a glow and character of its own, yet shares it with the interior space.

woods all around, with only bathroom and kitchen shielded, and the most private wing of Wheeler Kearn's Prairie house has windows floor to ceiling, with roll-up shades built in only to shade the sun, not the view of wandering foxes and wild turkeys.

The livability factor depends on transitions, too, including moving from outdoors to indoors, summer to winter, and work to play. It's always been a necessity, but today the mudroom takes a rightful stand as a prime space, and many of the best houses feature mudrooms of substantial size and fine design. Seasons are accounted for in the livable house, with landscaping providing shade in the summer, such as in Ted Montgomery's energy-friendly house, which made room for a tree growing through the greenhouse roof (photo facing page). And work and play each have designated space in a well-designed house, with accommodations for quiet and entertainment, solitude and community.

Craft: A Respect for Materials and Workmanship

The celebration of honest materials and fine craftsmanship may seem at first like icing on the cake compared to how well a house works and what it looks like from the curb. Imagine a house that's beautifully sited, nicely proportioned, and perfectly laid out. Then imagine giving it a closer look and finding that details are skimpy, materials are shoddy, and workmanship is lackluster. Crown molding with gaping joints, electrical outlets and switches positioned with no forethought, out-of-plumb framing and other aesthetic and functional annoyances can knock points off the fanciest house. Although the bones and guts of a house may not grab immediate attention, that's where craft is the most vital. No amount of caulk can permanently plug a leak caused by improper flashing.

When things go well, fine craftsmanship brings satisfaction to everyone involved. The beautifully crafted concrete countertop that tops the kitchen island in a rural California house is art in the hands of designer Fu-Tung Cheng but also utility to the owners who prepare dinner and take meals on

A DESIRE TO STAY IN TUNE with seasonal changes led to the decision to wrap an existing tree with greenhouse glazing. The skillful detailing of building materials not only makes such a detail work but also gives the house a delightful texture and shape from ground up.

the silky-smooth surface (photo below). The Craftsman-style detailing in Curtiss Gelotte's Seattle bungalow is a celebration of joinery, wood, and physics—and the spaces within are a delight to live in.

An understanding of and respect for the particular qualities of materials is fundamental to good craftsmanship. Building materials that are traditional to a region, such as adobe to the Southwest, are good choices because they respond directly to availability and climate. Yet the adobe house in Santa Fe, designed by Bauer, Freeman, McDermott Architects, has a completely different scale and ambience than the adobe house tucked into a Mexican hill town. House + House's Mexican retreat is urban, brightly colored, and dazzling with contrasting materials such as wrought iron, concrete, and glass (photo facing page), while Bauer's design is cool, elegant, and classical, yet both pay homage to traditional building materials and methods.

Good craftsmanship doesn't necessarily mean always using materials in a traditional way. Sometimes thinking outside the box can create a joint, a component, or a finish that's just the right touch. And don't despair that a big budget is key, either. The creative use of salvaged items can be the brainchild behind a design. One example is the cottage in Kansas, built for $50,000 from salvaged fink trusses, corrugated steel roofing, among other salvage-yard finds (photo p. 20). No hodgepodge of found objects, the design is a symmetrical, graceful, and well-crafted tribute to architect/builder Dan Rockhill's ingenuity and skill.

EXQUISITELY CRAFTED, well-proportioned architectural elements and the artful placement of windows and openings all come together to provide a big visual and spiritual impact in this California home for a growing family.

Distinctiveness: The "Wow" Factor

So, here's a house that should fit its site and owners like a glove and that was designed with an understanding of craft. Just one more step will take the house design up that last notch, from house to home, from being admirable to being loved. Whether it's a cottage or a compound, the house that wins affection always distinguishes itself with a personality—not a par-

IN THIS COURTYARD house, everything comes together with a sense of style that's both tranquil and festive. All elements—color and texture, light and shade, solitude and community—work together to make this a distinctive space.

ticular style but a sense of style. That distinctiveness, or "wow" factor, can relate to any of the other core qualities. The way a house is designed to fit in the landscape can provide the punch, such as Ralph Rapson's glass cube in the Wisconsin woods, where layers of structure and off-the-shelf windows and glass doors are composed to frame a view that's spectacular during storms and soothing at sunrise. The Napa Valley compound designed by Eric Haesloop draws on symmetry and proportion to guide not only the site plan but floor plans, elevations, and structural elements, with Douglas fir and stone providing the palette that transforms each space. The Shim Sutcliffe house, which hovers over a lake in Ontario, is a breathtaking composition made up of finely crafted wood, metal, glass, wrought with such finesse and rhythm that the house looks ready to set a course for the opposite shore.

The "nifty fifty" come from all over North America.

Certainly a spectacular view of water, woods, horizon, or city skyline does make it easier to build in "wow" factor. In fact, the insightful use of light and view are hallmarks of every great house. But there's more to making a distinctive house than going for a home run. Details, finishes, and the configuration of space can add whimsy, elegance, mystery, serenity—whatever quality is right for the space and place. And the smallest of details can add spice, such as the careful balance of color and line found in the mantel design of a Massachusetts house designed by Paul Lukez Architects.

Great Houses Are Everywhere

Studying these 50 great houses could lead to a sudden urge to pull up roots, or can lead to a discovery much closer to home. Northwest readers may be inspired by the houses in Oregon,

A CLEARING IN KANSAS provides the setting for a small house that is so much more than the sum of its salvaged parts. Glazing between the struts of the gable end trusses gives a jewel-box look at sunset and allows a peaceful view by day.

A SENSITIVE REMODEL preserved the clean lines and traditional shape of this 200-year-old New England cape.

Washington, and British Columbia, which range from a suburban Seattle bungalow painstakingly rendered in the Craftsman tradition by Curtiss Gelotte Architects to a very small but perfectly proportioned in-town house designed by Howard Davis. The farmhouse aficionado has a bushel of vernacular-inspired houses to study, among them Wheeler Kearn's sprawling rural compound with a view of Lake Michigan, Steve Atkinson's dog-trot cabin tucked in cool shade in Louisiana, and, in a historic town in Virginia, a white porch-trimmed house designed with new bones but an old heart by Versaci and Neumann.

Although geographic spread wasn't a constraint as the houses were reviewed, the "nifty fifty" came from all over North America, from coast to coast, and from forest and prairie to city center to suburban street. The wealth of variety in location—not to mention shape, size, and style—offers concrete proof that if the design is inspired, a great house can be built anywhere, including your own-neighborhood.

THE Houses

50 GREAT HOUSES

FROM

50 AMERICAN ARCHITECTS

A Traditional House
with Modern Composure

SPARE, DELICATE DETAILS pair with a subdued color palette to make a serene, elegant living room. Built-in cabinetry—including storage in the window seat—disguises a wealth of toys, CDs, games, and a stereo system.

I t's tempting to stick a label

on a house style, whether to make a sale or to ease the

process of finding complementary furnishings. But labels

can be both limiting and confusing. A

house with Colonial proportions and

details can be labeled traditional, but so

can a Victorian-style house or even a

post-and-beam house. And who's to say

The house is comfortable on its site.

that a traditional house has to be historically accurate from

foundation to chimney? This elegant house in a New York

City suburb could easily be labeled as traditional, but a

closer look reveals a modern nuance that keeps colors sub-

dued, spaces uncluttered, and details elegant and simple.

What gives the house its traditional flavor are the materi-

als and the detailing, such as painted clapboards and Doric-

style columns, cabinetry with inset drawers and doors, and

divided-light windows. What creates a modern overtone is

THE LINEAR RHYTHMS established by white Doric-style columns, clapboards, and rafters are balanced by the dark accents of copper gutters, downspouts, and light fixtures.

A CAPACIOUS MUDROOM has room for everyone, even the family dog, who goes in and out by way of a Plexiglas® entry; the solid top-hinged door can be easily closed and bolted. High-gloss paint on wainscoting and a bluestone floor make durable finishes in a high-traffic room.

Architect:
Dennis Wedlick, AIA
Location:
New York State

Dark stain on the oak plank floor and the heavy, ornate door make a sophisticated contrast to the white walls and wainscoting. The black spiral stair, which leads from the study down to the mudroom, adds a modern touch, while the attic-bound ladder lends a nautical flavor.

The ample mudroom has space for a potting corner, complete with sink, and storage for gardening tools and boots. Even though it's a mere mudroom, this space receives the same attention to details, color, and materials that are found throughout.

Just off the kitchen, the pantry is as elegant as a kitchen, with beautifully crafted inset doors and drawers and open cabinets above. The abundant storage is supplemented by countertops that provide workspace.

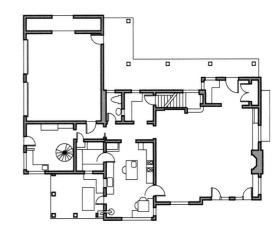

restraint—spaces are large but not heavily embellished, and window treatments steer clear of the elaborate fabrics often found in a large, elegant house. Black metal elements such as the spiral stair, the curtain rods, and exterior light fixtures are used throughout to add a modern—as in early-20th-century Modern—touch. What makes the joining of traditional and modern work so well is the superb crafts-manship throughout, from the beautifully executed copper gutters and downspouts to the finely crafted cabinetry.

But style alone doesn't make for livability. Despite its large overall size, this house doesn't have that too-big-for-its-site look that new suburban houses too often have. Thanks to an L-shaped plan and a roofline that's broken up, the house looks comfortable on its site. Rooms are generous but not too large, and plenty of space is given over to pedes-trian but essential spaces such as the mudroom and hallways. There are two sets of stairs, one a spacious straight run and one a spiral stair; these are well lit by windows to com-plete the gracious, cheerful effect.

IN THE MASTER BEDROOM, a window seat with storage below tucks into a tiny nook between the fireplace and a corner built-in. A wall of French doors bathes the room in light.

Shipshape on Martha's Vineyard

*Some homes are just
"-less"—timeless,
affectless, and effortless.
With a gentle nestling
of its form and spaces
in the landscape, this
simple plan literally
melts into its setting.*

DUO DICKINSON

TUCKED AMONG TREES
AT THE TOP OF A HILL,
this family house on
Martha's Vineyard looks
ever seaward. Deep over-
hangs and a long porch
roof screen the southern
sun yet allow for long
views.

Sometimes summer makes

the living so easy that seasonal visitors are seduced into island living year-round. This new house on Martha's Vineyard is the product of such a move. The land itself has been in the family for years, with a small cottage that suited temporary, seasonal living. But a full-time commitment to the island required a house with space and finishes that could stand up to 365 days of use each year, not only by its regular inhabitants but also by a stream of visitors. The imagery remains that of a seaside house, no longer cottage-sized but boat-sized. A curved wraparound deck, long horizontal lines, and nautical proportions recall the ferries that travel hourly between the mainland and Martha's Vineyard.

In line with today's trend of joining cooking, eating, and living spaces, this house has a long great room that looks out over the porch, hillside, and sea

More refined than its summer sister.

Architect:
Peter Breese, AIA
Breese Architects
Location:
Martha's Vineyard, Massachusetts

THE ENTIRE SOUTH WALL of the living room is home to a generous window seat, deep enough for taking a snooze and wide enough to accommodate family and friends. Casement windows let in the sea breeze.

A CURVED BENCH finishes the deck like the bow of a ship, an image that suits this seaside house. Shingles and structure were allowed to weather to gray, while window frames and door frames are finished to resist weathering.

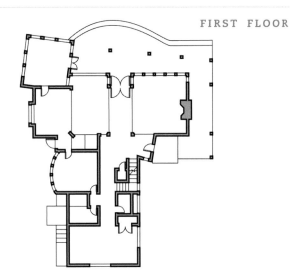

This outdoor shower is both a charming garden folly and a vital tool for keeping sand and dirt from beach and garden out of the house. It is located next to a stair that leads to the upstairs laundry and bathroom.

far below. To keep the room from appearing simply big and undifferentiated, oriental carpets divide up the space, a long window-seat alcove adds intimacy and focus to the living room, and the ceiling over the kitchen is lowered. To balance the large public space, and to keep the television out of constant view, a family room near the kitchen takes on the role of media center and teen retreat. In a similar manner, children have ample space in bedrooms for friends and cousins, but built-in cozy spaces allow for privacy.

A year-round house often takes on a more refined air than its summer sister. Here, traces of rustic living appear in the form of a partly exposed post-and-beam structure and exposed floor joists, but exposed lumber is painted to add a layer of refinement. A beadboard wainscoting recalls walls in a seaside summer cottage, but the beadboard is painted and capped with an elaborate molding. Still, a front-and-center tire swing and a charming, spiral-fenced outdoor shower are reminders even in the winter that this is still a summer place.

Sisters don't mind sharing a room with so many cozy and exciting spaces to be in. The built-in structure that holds beds, bookcases, and sleeping lofts is painted in parts and covered with easy-to-clean plastic laminate in others.

 in the house, this kitchen pass-through makes it easy to dine on the porch and keeps cooks and loungers in touch.

COOKING, DINING, AND LIVING SPACES are side by side in one great room, but the character of each space is individually defined by rugs, walls, windows, and ceiling heights. Parts of the structure are exposed for variety but painted for refinement.

A Timber Frame Redressed

The stunning trick here is the architect's ability to preserve the original character of the house while reinterpreting the historic timber frame to accommodate a contemporary lifestyle.

JOHN CONNELL

THE 200-YEAR-OLD OAK TIMBER FRAME is the sole survivor of an extensive overhaul. A fourth bedroom was left out of the redo to create this two-story space, leaving a comfortable 1,750 sq. ft. The call for more windows to counter the long winter nights is evident in this first-floor wall of windows, spaced apart to make room for artwork.

I t was never in the cards to demolish

this house, which is just a few years younger than the United States Constitution and 40 years older than its home state of Maine. But it was tempting, as 200 years of use showed on every surface, and spaces felt especially cramped and dark. Yet there was historical value in the house, though not in the details or in the arrangement of rooms or its place in the landscape. What counted in this house was the structure itself, a stalwart timber frame with good proportions, intact joinery, and enough amplitude to hang a new skin on. So everything but the frame was stripped—partitions, lath and plaster, floor joists and flooring, windows and doors. What could be salvaged, such as casement windows, was saved.

A simple 4-ft. bumpout adds multitudes to the kitchen.

In the first stage of its new life, the timber frame was scrubbed with a wire brush and oiled, then filled in with fewer walls, larger—and fewer—rooms, a two-story space, and a better way to relate to its wooded site with a river view. In place of the diminutive vestibule that was just off the living room, a deck with

Architect:
Robert Knight, AIA
Knight Associates, Architects
Location:
Maine

A SNOWY EVENING makes plain the reason for sticking with the old bones and traditional shape of a 200-year-old New England cape.

FORMERLY HOME to a couple of saddleback sheds, this side of the reworked house now features the entryway, with welcoming bench and extended roof. New windows on both floors add style to the façade.

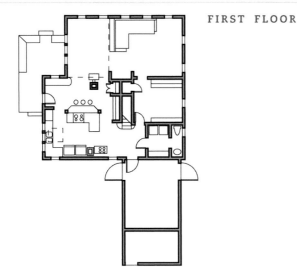

CASEMENTS SALVAGED FROM the demolished skin of the house are reused in the main bedroom and in the bathroom. A high window in the opposite wall extends the view.

THE LARGEST OF THE THREE BEDROOMS is tucked under the gabled roof but is still well lit by a skylight, a gable-end light, and light from the reused casement windows, which also help funnel heat upstairs.

two benches makes a welcoming entry, with a front door that opens onto an alcove beside the kitchen. A bench for shoe changing and hooks for coats are handier and tidier than the cramped closet of old. A simple 4-ft. bumpout adds multitudes to the efficiency and grace of the kitchen, which is now big enough for two cooks.

The knockout punch is the combined living and dining space, and the decision to leave off the fourth bedroom upstairs to give the dining space a two-story advantage. The house is heated by two woodstoves, and this tall space funnels just enough heat upstairs. As a gesture to the house that was, the old casement windows have a new home in the largest bedroom and the bathroom, both overlooking the two-story space. The windows offer views of the action below, help with air circulation, and, best of all, allow a line of sight to the woods and river beyond.

MOVING THE KITCHEN WALL 4 ft. back made a much more generous space for working and made room for a new front door, seen in the background at left. A bench and hooks take the place of a closet. The timber frame is exposed where possible, but joists and floorboards are paneled over with drywall to avoid dust seeping down on dinner.

NEW MEETS OLD in the kitchen, with modern appliances and lighting coexisting with traditional inset cabinets with porcelain knobs.

A Cottage Takes Root in the Maine Woods

WHY THIS HOUSE

Like a delicate piece of embroidery, this cottage is part of a seamless flow between the forest and the house. You want to ask, is it new or old? The very question says it all.

JEREMIAH ECK

A NEWCOMER TO THIS FOREST COTTAGE in Maine could easily believe the house has been here for decades, as its shape, finishes, details, and siting give it the air of timelessness.

THIS SLIM CROSS-GABLED WING is home to the living-room window seat, which has an enviable panorama of the woods through three tall divided-light windows.

W hether the product of fairy tales or family camping trips, there's something lingering from childhood that makes a cottage in the woods an enchanting place. Part of it is sensory: a forest setting of cool shadows and dappled light, the sound of birds and rustling of little animals, the smell of a wood fire and a glimpse of smoke drifting from a chimney, rough stone walls and

A window-seat alcove receives singular treatment.

smooth-planed wood. Adding to the charm is the separation from town life and the consequent sloughing off of stress and commotion. That, and size: A smaller house not only allows for more focus on small details but offers built-in coziness.

This twin-gabled cottage in Maine fits perfectly in its grove of hardwoods, but because of foresight, not luck. The house was positioned carefully so that few trees had to be removed, and construction was carried out with an eye to maintaining the existing plant life. Once the house was finished, the owners planted its

Architect:
James Sterling, AIA
James Sterling Architect
Location:
Naples, Maine

THIS WINDOW-SEAT ALCOVE gets its magical feel from the windows and the peaceful view, but also from the way the ceiling follows the gabled roof and is washed in light. The wall continues across the opening to make a defined frame.

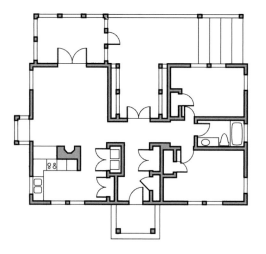

RATHER THAN THE USUAL LUMBERYARD LATTICE, a phalanx of pickets makes a tidy screen for the deck and screened-porch foundation. A slim line of wood decking adds a golden color contrast to the green woodwork. Railing posts are beveled to match gables and shed water quickly.

edges and the edges of a path cut to a nearby lake with shade-loving flora indigenous to New England forests. Colors and materials reflect those in the woods, with a special affinity for spring and fall: green trim and gable siding, slate-colored roof shingles, and cedar shingles dipped in clear preservative to retain their natural color. As a result, the house looks as if it's been there a century.

Inside, the twin-gable arrangement allows private and public to stay at arm's length, divided by a central entry hall with direct access to the back porches. Because the cottage is small and the woods are dense, special attention was paid to making the house light. Pickled cedar ceiling boards, light oak floors, white walls, and plenty of windows keep the house airy, as do the ceilings, which follow the gables up so that spaces look larger.

Three types of windows give the cottage complexity and meaning. Gable ends and the kitchen window are fitted with large, square, four-light awning windows, which help with ventilation even in rain, while most other windows are traditional double-hungs with divided upper sashes. A window-seat alcove receives the singular treatment of three tall, narrow, multipaned windows, giving the space a spiritual nature that suits the peace of the forest.

DESPITE ITS DIMINUTIVE SIZE, the cottage boasts a spacious, welcoming living room, made gracious by the high ceiling and massive, soaring granite fireplace. The kitchen, behind the fireplace, is well lit by its own double-hung and awning windows but it also borrows light from the living room over the bookcase.

Cool, Calm, and Composed

SHINY GALVANIZED ROOFING, crisp white clapboards, and neat rows of windows distinguish these house elements as ordered, man-made objects in a natural setting of forest, field, and ocean. At left is a studio, in the center a barn for cars and tools, and at right the house proper. A broad metal shed roof shades first-floor windows on the southwest side.

Interior spaces are as crisp and serene as the outside.

The water's edge is seductive

for its drama, but it's not always the ideal place to build a house. The owner of this coastal home in New England felt that the water's edge was a special place to go, not to build on, so the house sits high on a meadow overlooking the water. Curiously, the house has an even more dramatic impact than it would if it hugged the shore. Its "wow" factor comes from the relationship of three distinct house parts to each other and to the site. The three structures pinwheel around a courtyard to make a composition that is at once more complex than a single building and more in scale with the landscape. Two low stone walls extend from the main house to distinguish the built from the natural.

Architect:
Elliott Elliott Norelius Architecture
Location:
Coastal Maine

THE SUN-FILLED LIVING ROOM has high ceilings and long vistas, and plentiful windows take advantage of both. In Maine, the sun is a welcome commodity—most of the time. This late-morning sun is pleasant, and a long view of the bay rules out window shades.

ALIGNED WITH THE ENTRY of the main house, a path of irregular-shaped stones leads the way to the studio. A broad metal awning, its underside visible here, shades sun in summer and shields snow in winter.

41

THE STUDIO IS STUDDED with tiny corner windows that throw beams of light across walls all day; a tall, narrow window behind the woodstove takes in a view of the vegetable garden and woods. Narrow window casing keeps the frame secondary and the prized view foremost.

THERE'S A SHAKER-MEETINGHOUSE SIMPLICITY about the main building, with its unassuming gable roof, stone base, and divided-light windows. But a few details add a modern twist, such as metal-wrapped chimneys, French doors, and a squad of arms-akimbo deck chairs.

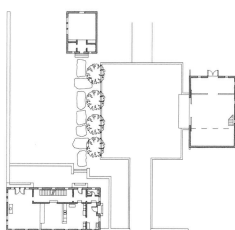

The main house, tallest of the three, is turned gable end to the shore and broadside to the two smaller buildings; it has an abundance of windows and generous stone terraces on two sides. Both studio and barn are studded with tiny clerestory windows that add texture and spots of light. All three buildings are clad with crisp white clapboards, white trim, and galvanized steel roofing. Although clearly not designed to blend with the landscape, this house is built in a region of abundant snow, so in winter the buildings fit into the landscape like an arctic fox.

Inside spaces are designed to be as serene and crisp as the outside, with the landscape in view from all sides. Windows are plentiful, and although there are no window walls, as in a modern-style house, spare furnishings and architectural elements give the house a contemporary air. The stone-slab fireplace with stainless-steel chimney pipe sits apart like a sculptural object between two large windows facing the bay. Between each pair of windows, and in other cool spots in the houses, two dozen silver radiators march along, kin to the silver-colored roofs on the three buildings.

A LAUNDRY ROOM between dressing room and bedrooms is bright and cheery, with storage for linens and toiletries immediately at hand. Front-loading machines allow for a granite top for folding, and a not-so-utilitarian utility sink can serve for hand laundry or washing hands.

A Seaside House Bares Its Bones

WHY THIS HOUSE

Inventive detailing and creative construction methods are the ingredients for this coastline retreat, which feels like a huge boat hull inverted against the weather. Residential architecture doesn't get much better.

JOHN CONNELL

THIS NOVA SCOTIA CABIN is a prime spot for bird-watching and enjoying the waters of Eel Bay. The shingled wood skin of the house and the pine decking have weathered to gray in the salt air, and the curved roof and tiny punched window add to the nautical look.

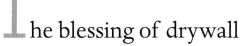

The blessing of drywall

is that it often covers a confusion of wires and a crooked regiment of studs, leaving a clean, smooth surface to decorate. But the guts of a house can, if well considered and well wrought, be a thing of beauty. In this coastal Nova Scotia cabin, economy required that the bare necessities get built first, with partitions, finishes, and embellishments following as the budget allowed. After living with exposed studs and wiring, however, the owners chose to leave the structure uncovered and augment the cabin to match. It helped that their architect has a bent for boatbuilding, in which structural elements are admired not only for utility but also for beauty.

Wood structural elements and details give the house its character, from curved, laminated roof beams to

Prevailing winds influenced the house's skin.

BUDGET CONSTRAINTS called for this bayside house to be finished in stages, with the shell and utilities of the house built first and the finishes added later. But the owners grew to love the patterns of the exposed structure and the way the color and detail complemented the natural landscape of woods and water.

IN A NATURAL SETTING, sheltered outdoor space is important year-round. Early mornings, the deck is a shady retreat, but much of the day it's a boon to sunbathers—or in turbulent weather, home to fearless storm watchers.

Architect:
Brian MacKay-Lyons Architect
Location:
Nova Scotia

45

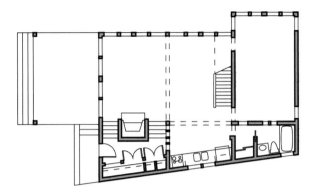

BECAUSE THE HOUSE IS OFF THE ELECTRICAL GRID and required generators to power tools, most structural elements were built off site and quickly assembled on site. Curved, laminated beams, horizontal cribbing, and square plywood panels give the house the quality of a boat under construction.

grids created by horizontal and vertical wood slats, such as those surrounding the fireplace or forming the stair railing. While the house appears simple at first, there's a spatial diversity that adds vitality to the craftsmanship. The roof is curved, but this is no mere half-barrel vault. The east wall angles out to give the curved roof more complexity, like part of the hull of a ship. The plan is divided into four equal bays—deck, entry / living, kitchen / dining, and bedroom / bath—but the angled east wall and bedroom pop-out add a dynamic that keeps the house fresh.

It's not just the joy of messing about in boats that gives the house character. The proximity of Eel Bay and the direction of prevailing winds influenced not only the placement of the house amid a grove of trees, but also the nature of the house's skin. Southwest walls facing the bay and the Atlantic Ocean beyond are built of posts, beams, and glass, while the northeast walls, which face the woods, are shingled, with few windows. Although the house is set in a grassy rise and surrounded by trees, floor-to-ceiling windows and glass doors running the length of two sides make the house seem perched on the edge of a cliff, or even afloat at sea.

A NONCOMBUSTIBLE HEARTH and decorative wood cribbing flank this zero-clearance metal fireplace. On each side of the fireplace, steps lead down to the entryway. Raising the living level above the entry saves energy in colder climates, as cool air stays low.

OPEN SHELVES ARE SUPPORTED BY STUDS in the wall between kitchen and entryway, allowing light to flow and dishes to become decorative elements. The fireplace cribbing beyond has a lobster-trap quality.

THE LIVING AND DINING/KITCHEN SPACES are left open and undefined by walls or niches, which allows spaces to serve any function. This private reading nook suits the early afternoon, but it can easily become a communal corner for watching the sun set after a summer dinner.

Easy on the Earth,
Easy on the Eyes

Unlike many early solar houses, this one is both sustainable and beautifully designed. And the owner-architect has managed it all without compromising his circus-like penchant for design and merriment.

JOHN CONNELL

COLOR IS A MAJOR DESIGN ELEMENT in the living room. The purple back wall and green built-in plywood shelves are complementary colors in the same tone, making them harmonious but not humdrum. The custom-made couch can be pulled apart into single seats, while the love seat is one piece with plywood backs that double as pockets for magazines or blankets.

THIS SOUTH-FACING INDOOR-OUTDOOR GARDEN ROOM is the hub of the house. Living spaces and bedrooms open onto the garden room to take advantage of the light, heat, and view that it offers. The soft green color of the wall makes the space blend with the plants when viewed from outside the house.

Envision 13 houses on 88 acres

of land in New England. It's likely the image is of large homes, each surrounded by a vast lawn, massive trees and shrubbery, and a tall stone wall—not exactly a picture of community. Instead, this community development near Burlington, Vermont, is a pleasant surprise. Here, 13 houses take up only 8 acres, with the remaining 80 acres dedicated as common space, part of which is wooded, part left open. Homeowners determined how their individual houses would look and how they would be oriented. This house is sited for energy efficiency, designed with sustainable materials, and overlaid with a sense of humor and delight.

A south-facing garden space is both inside and out.

The house faces east and south toward the beneficial sun. A garage shields the north side against winter winds,

Architect:
Ted Montgomery
GroundSwell Architects
Location:
Burlington, Vermont

THIS HOME FITS PERFECTLY into its wooded setting overlooking the community's green space. The homeowners chose to have a subtle labyrinth sculpted into the grass.

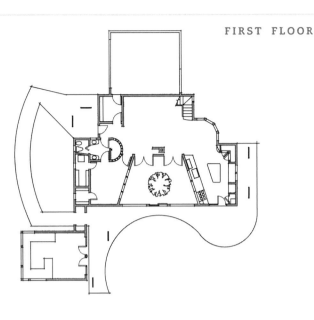

THE 75-FT. WHITE ASH growing through the roof is one of many left on the site, and it symbolizes the focus on sustainable design. All trees that had to be cut down were milled into finish lumber for use inside the house.

and earth is mounded against the north and west sides to minimize the effect of weather on the house. At the center of the layout is a south-facing garden space that is both indoors and out, with a tall preexisting ash tree growing through the glass roof, a hose bib for watering the abundant plants, and decking that allows for drainage. Living spaces and bedrooms overlook this space and share in its light, heat, view, and fresh air. A studio to the southwest not only shields the garden room from wind but also creates a large, sheltered courtyard just outside the garden, further defined by a lovely trellis gateway between studio and house.

Materials and details are a blend of economy and whimsy, with careful attention to ecologically sensitive materials such as formaldehyde-free particleboard, nontoxic paint, and heat-retaining concrete floors stained to look like leather. Designed and built by the owner/architect, the furniture, cabinetry, and railings are brightly painted and embellished with charming cutouts and curves, adding a light touch to a serious intent.

IN A HOUSE WITH BIG GESTURES, whimsical shapes, and bright colors, the window seat provides a retreat of sorts. Its ceiling is low, colors are subdued, and textures are soft, making it ideal for reading, looking outdoors, or having tea.

COPPER TUBING makes a gloriously curvy balustrade that recalls late-19th-century art nouveau ironwork.

THE CHILDREN'S BATHROOM is a collage of gently contrasting shapes, colors, and textures. Rough, rectilinear concrete block abuts a smooth, shiny copper countertop, copper tubing, and flatpanel curve-topped drawers painted a soft matte green.

A Classical Perspective
on a Romantic Setting

A CLASSICAL VILLA in shape but a farmhouse in attire, this Connecticut house is both welcoming and formal. White gates attached to the foreground outbuildings can close off the courtyard.

A house in the country can be rustic,

earth-toned, rambling, organic, informal—or none of the above. This rural house in Connecticut makes no attempt to blend with the landscape. Instead, it's an object in the landscape, and a lovely one at that. Both plan and elevations are unabashedly symmetrical, and the site plan is formal, with a central courtyard and matching outbuildings standing guard at the entry, much like a classical villa. But the formality is leavened by references to the rural vernacular, such as white walls clad with smooth, white vertical-board siding, flat red shingles on the roof, the paired farmhouse gates attached to the outbuildings, and the farmhouse-style porches on the house's back side.

The same geometric treatment that orders the overall layout of the house is carried into every level of the design.

Rhythmic elements intertwine with light and space.

Squares, rectangles, and triangles abut and align to make corresponding rhythms on

Architect:
Centerbrook Architects and Planners
Location:
Connecticut

THE BACK OF THE HOUSE maintains a clean, classical look, but with the amendments of more casual elements, such as farmhouse-style porches and a wonderfully tangled trumpet creeper vine.

THE SAME ATTENTION TO GEOMETRIC PATTERNS that infuses the house with character is applied to the fireplace mantel in the family room.

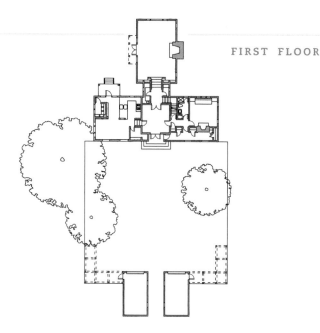

walls, ceilings, trim, and details such as shutters and light fixtures. These cadences are far from rigid or overwhelming; in fact, rhythmic elements intertwine with light and space to make comfortable, glowing spaces and work to frame lovely views.

The most dramatic view, from the living room, was only discovered when the owners began clearing much of the woods to return the hillside to farm fields, as it had been a century before. Many handsome stone walls were uncovered, but the bonanza was a breathtaking view across the valley to a mountain. The house is deliberately sited so that the mountain is visible from the beginning of the long driveway, then slips out of view behind the house itself, only coming back into view through the large living-room window.

THIS LARGE WINDOW is not only a focus for the view of fields and the distant mountain, but also a focus within the room, aligning with the trusses. The two grand pianos are used during frequent recitals.

DIVIDING THIS LARGE LIVING-ROOM WINDOW into squares and identically sized rectangles not only forms a pleasing pattern but also makes the window less overwhelming in size. The window is centered on the primary axis of the house and the site.

THE ENTRYWAY IS A GRACIOUS, LIGHT-FILLED HUB for each wing of the house. Custom woodwork is a hallmark throughout, from the triangle molding to the lattice light fixture, just in view.

SUBDUED GREEN AND RED STRIPES and painted scissors trusses add a medieval look to the living-room ceiling. These, plus flat trim applied to the ceiling and radiating from the trusses, play up the height of the room while making the space more comfortable.

Treading Lightly on the Dunes

IT'S HARD TO BUILD ON THE WIDE-OPEN COAST without being seen, but this Martha's Vineyard house keeps a humble profile while fitting in with local materials, colors, and proportions.

A site shapes the design

of a house by virtue of the physical—the climate, the terrain, the vegetation, and the fabric of surrounding buildings—but also by the less tangible constraints of law. A beachfront site, such as this one on Martha's Vineyard, is subject not only to local zoning regulations and building codes but also to federal and state coastal management. Good regulations come about from experience with both Mother Nature and human nature, so it makes sense to deem them essential to good design.

The space is broken into two square pavilions.

The shape taken by this beach house was first dictated by several legal constraints. The size and configuration were determined by the footprint of an existing fisherman's shack, and floodplain restrictions required that the first floor be 5 ft. above the ground. The architect felt that a two-story house would be too conspicuous, especially if the roof were sloped in traditional fashion. What could have been a drawback became a boon; the single

Architect:
Phil Regan
Mark Hutker Associates
Location:
Martha's Vineyard, Massachusetts

LIVING, DINING, AND COOKING SPACES fit into one large area under one of the hipped roofs. Keeping the house on a single level allowed each room to have a dramatic sloped ceiling and banks of windows, elements that add space and light to a modest footprint.

MASSING THE HOUSE into two separate buildings not only allows the roof to be lower and less obtrusive but also gives the house the look of having been built over time.

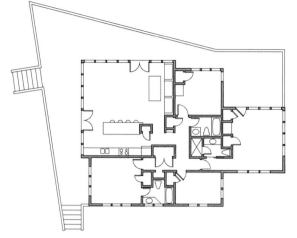

level provides all rooms with high, sloped ceilings, making for brighter, bigger spaces.

To further break up the mass of the house, the space is broken into two square pavilions with individual hipped roofs. The house is considered a "camp" and hence an informal, simple place to live, so the living/cooking/dining space is one big room fit into one square. A master bedroom fits into the second square, and three smaller bedrooms fit between the two big spaces. The double-square layout allows each bedroom to have a corner with two walls of windows overlooking sea and sand. In keeping with the goal of fitting quietly into the landscape, trim, shingles, and siding are stained with bleaching oil to bring out the natural gray.

THE MASTER BEDROOM ENJOYS A WIDE VIEW, thanks to a corner full of windows. The sill is dropped to extend the view, except adjacent to the bed, where more enclosure is preferred. Clerestory windows brighten the high ceiling.

IN THE MASTER BEDROOM, a built-in bureau fits between two closets with seaworthy economy and elegance.

THE LIVING SPACE HAS WINDOWS from the ceiling to just above the floor to take in the ocean view. The deck railing is designed with a simple wood frame and thin stainless-steel cables so it doesn't block the view from inside or out.

DIVIDING SPACES INTO TWO PAVILIONS allowed for two lower, hipped roofs rather than one massive roof. This gives the house the character of an inviting, charming camp rather than a castle by the sea.

A House of the Woods

WHY THIS HOUSE

If Louis XIV had built in the Northern Forest, he might have used this floor plan and these ceiling heights. Here's proof that woodland homes don't have to be rustic and roughhewn to respond to their context.

JOHN CONNELL

AT ONCE THE MOST SOPHISTICATED and the most natural room in the house, the screened porch is also the most lived in. With the elegance of a drawing room, it is dignified by an 18-ft.-high ceiling, thick columns, and tall French doors but kept casual by comfortable furniture, broad screened panels, and the nearness of the woods.

A ny number of images can inspire

the design for a house in the woods. A common

theme is a post-and-beam structure, making

reference to the tree as support and shelter. Rustic

textures, natural woods, and forest colors reinforce

the idea that the house belongs in

the wild. A captivating variation on

the theme of reflecting the woods

is found in this New Hampshire

house, which is thoroughly sophis-

ticated yet completely in tune

The screened porch is too elegant for such a name.

with its rocky, forested, and ungroomed site.

Cedar shingles, which weather to the subdued

colors of tree bark, cover the house from roof to

wall, save for several columns and the foundation,

built from stone to merge with the rocky ground.

Shingles even wrap window jambs and heads in

some places, adding depth to walls. The grayed

blue-green of spruces is replicated in the color of

Architect:
Charles Warren, AIA
Location:
New Hampshire

DARK AND HANDSOME, this New Hampshire house fits perfectly into its stony wooded site. Shingles cover the house head to toe and even wrap around sills and jams to give the wall depth. The tower contains the stair and bay alcove; a stone corner of the tall screened porch is at left.

THIS WINDOW, tucked into the corner, is worth two full-sized windows as light bounces off both wall and ceiling.

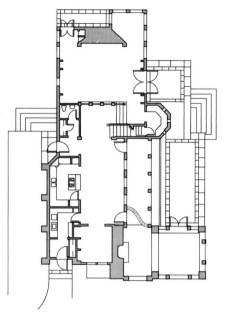

trim and piers; low-luster paint was chosen for its natural look. Shingled houses near the shore are often trimmed with white, a cheerful choice that looks clean and scrubbed. But white would have been glaring for this shingle house in the forest, even though it's on the shore of a lake. The dark shadows made by overhangs and dark-trimmed windows help the house look natural in the woodland shadows.

Inside, the house is far from rustic, but still in keeping with its image as a house in the woods. There's little dry-wall in sight, as wood covers walls in the form of panels or beadboard, painted a creamy white to add brightness.

The floor of alternating stripes of oak and maple shimmers in the diffuse light from the many windows. It's impossible to pin down one prize space or element of the house. There's a glorious staircase with a curved stringer and a massive living-room fireplace with deftly laid irregular stones. The two-story screened porch is far too elegant for such a mundane name, and a delightful alcove under the stair beckons with its own cozy, glowing ambience.

TUCKED BEHIND THE STAIR but by no means a leftover space, the bay alcove is a favorite corner. Walls covered with wood trim or paneling and carved-leg benches lend the look of a finely crafted state room. Windows are not large yet let in abundant light.

A STRAIGHT SCREEN WALL would have been simpler to build, but what a difference a curve makes. This undulating screen looks both airy and sturdy, with slender mullions for lightness and a wide frame for brawn. The porch beyond is outdoors.

INCORPORATING AN ELEGANT CURVED STRINGER and a dramatic straight run with a long, unattached balustrade, the staircase is a focal point of the interior. Oak tops treads and balustrade, while other elements are painted the same satin off-white as the rest of the house.

A CAREFULLY CRAFTED MASONRY SURROUND is rustic yet refined, with irregular stones joined as neatly as a jigsaw puzzle. Handsome cabinetry and a mix of formal and casual furniture round out the comfortable living room.

Recreating the Past at Water's Edge

Combining the comfort of the familiar and the delight of the unexpected, this home captures the essence of New England architecture.

DUO DICKINSON

AT TWILIGHT, this house on the coast of Maine delivers the look of a century-old cottage with gabled dormers and a wraparound, shed-roofed porch. Exterior colors imitate the colors of trees, stones, sky, and water. The gable-end facade features a first-floor exterior wall that swells out slightly to give a boatlike look to the cottage.

I t's not easy to build a house

along the water, as lots are rare, costs are high, and codes are strict. So coastal-house hunters often buy an existing house to fulfill their waterside dream. That was the case with this coastal house in Maine, except that the existing house was a log cabin that had stood almost a century, only to be burnt to the ground after a lightning strike shortly after it was sold. The new owners had no time to mourn, as ordinances required that any new house on the site be under construction within 18 months, or the land on that rocky peninsula would be off limits for building.

Port Orford cedar steps have an ageless look.

The cabin that had burned down had been in the previous owners' family for generations, so the new owners felt the replacement cottage should recreate the spirit of that family retreat. Requirements to follow the identical footprint and maintain the same volume were not seen as constraints but as guidelines for making a better fit to the site. Traditional 19th-century American cottage elements fine-tuned the shape

Architect:
Stephen Blatt, AIA
Stephen Blatt Architects
Location:
Long Lake, Maine

THE APPROACH TO THIS NEW COTTAGE has no attached garage to spoil the atmosphere of a retreat. Visitors enter either the red-framed front door or the more informal door to the green-framed screened porch.

PAINTED-WOOD ELEMENTS ARE COLORFUL but not brassy, as the darker shades match tones found in the landscape. Openings between porch rafters allow light indoors, while the shallow pitch makes this modern detail barely visible from a distance. The kneewall gives a clear-cut visual edge to the porch and buffers strong breezes.

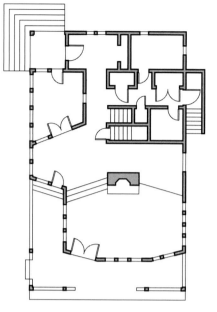

of the house, including the steeply pitched gable with multiple-gabled dormers and the broad wraparound porch.

Of course, today's houses offer some design features that can't be passed up, such as windows in all shapes and sizes. Modern windows are often larger than their antique counterparts due to improvements in energy efficiency and manufacturing techniques—and because the view is a precious commodity. Large, single-pane windows would look out of scale on this cottage, so it made sense to group smaller windows and include divided lights in the upper sash. Another modern element is the open plan, with the dining and living spaces separated by steps, not a door. And the generous wraparound front steps are much more expansive than the simple wood tread-and-railing stair found on an old cottage. Though new, these gray Port Orford cedar steps have an ageless look, reminiscent of the gray stones piled at the water's edge.

TALL PINE BEADBOARD WAINSCOTING runs through the house; here it's painted a soft blue-green. The window is a handsome composition, with an arched, fixed divided-light window atop two large awning windows and a straight, beaded head casing—a less expensive yet more graceful design than the predictable curved casing.

ONE WAY TO SET SPACE APART is to make the ceiling of a large space higher, but that can conflict with a second floor. Here, a higher ceiling is created by sinking the living room a few steps down, a strategy that makes the house seem to step down to the water.

ANYONE WOULD LOVE TO SLEEP in an attic-shaped room if it had this much light and charm. The room is small, but the steep gable, white paint, and generous window make the space feel both large and cozy.

A House in Tune

What's so wonderful about this house is its self-control. It's a great example of fitting into an existing neighborhood yet standing out as an example of thoughtful, up-to-date design.

JEREMIAH ECK

THE FAMILY ROOM FIRE-PLACE represents the design principles that created this house. Balance of materials, colors, and shapes is determined by the Golden Mean (a ratio of 1:1.6)—not by symmetry or happenstance. Colors are subtle but rich, and precision is leavened by whimsy.

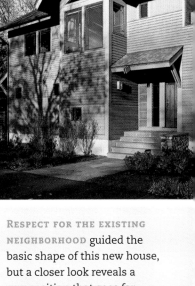

It happens all the time in hot real estate markets: Someone buys a modest older house, knocks it down, and builds a new house twice the size. It makes sense, as building new is often cheaper and speedier than adding on or renovating, and homeowners can get the space and amenities they desire. Unfortunately, the new, overblown house is often not only out of scale with the neighborhood, but also a stylistic alien. This replacement house in Lexington, Massachusetts, is an exception.

Color adds jazz to the arrangement.

What makes this new stand-in a good neighbor in its 1960s development is that the shape and details of the house emulate the predominant split-level style. The entryway is raised a few steps, a shallow-pitch gable faces front, and windows are high and grouped in pairs to look horizontal. To provide more room and still keep the street façade in sync with the neighborhood, a large L-shaped wing extends into the backyard, well hidden from the street by trees. This wing also creates a private terrace like that adjoining an urban townhouse—an unusual and pleasant addition

Architect:
Paul Lukez, AIA
Paul Lukez Architecture
Location:
Lexington, Massachusetts

RESPECT FOR THE EXISTING NEIGHBORHOOD guided the basic shape of this new house, but a closer look reveals a composition that goes far beyond the ordinary. It is evident in the placement of windows and window mullions themselves, and in the artful arrangement of trim and three types of siding to make a base, middle, and top.

THIS ENTRYWAY IS A STUDY IN LIGHT AND GEOMETRY. The door is sectioned with asymmetric, alternating-grain wood panels, while sidelight and copper panels together are the same width as the door.

ALONG THE SOUTHEAST WALL of the living room, which faces the courtyard and backyard, both wall and ceiling open up to bring in abundant light and view.

A CORNER OF THE KITCHEN opens onto the family room, which is two steps down. The extra height gives the family room a more spacious feel, and a diagonal sight line, such as this one from the dining room, makes the expanse look larger than it is.

A METAL TUBE RAILING in a commercial building would take a sharp jog here, a homely but necessary transition to keep the handrail at regulation height. This graceful railing is split in two, with each rail embracing the wood-slatted wall.

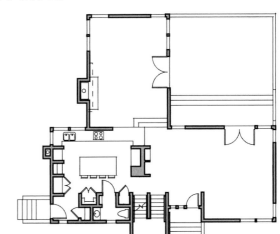

to a suburban backyard. A detached garage offers convenience without adding bulk to the house itself.

What elevates the design far above the average split-level house is the artful way finishes, windows, and trim are composed to balance each other on several levels, from the arrangement of window mullions to the organization of windows and trim across the façade. Color adds jazz to the arrangement by way of thin, bright window trim, moss-green paneling and siding, and paler, blue-toned trim. This attention to detail and joy in the pleasure of composition makes its way into the house, especially at the fireplace and the kitchen, where stone, metal, and wood surpass their utility as finishes to become beautifully crafted sculptural elements.

A SPLIT-LEVEL BACKSPLASH pays homage to the 1960s house style, but with considerably more sophistication. Acid-treated copper and aluminum panels behind and over the cooktop repeat the proportion of the windows, with a large pane flanked by a narrow one. Cherry cabinets make a warm-toned backdrop for sparkling glass and metal panels.

A Comfortable Fit on the New England Coast

WHY THIS HOUSE

Understated design and warm materials make this house a real home, integrated with the landscape and comfortable to live in. A subtle twist of the bedroom wing helps both to define the entry and open the living/dining areas to better views of the water.

JEREMIAH ECK

THE HOUSE FACES SOUTH AND EAST over the bay—a wonderful view but one that needs shading from the sun at times. Broad sunshades protect corner bedrooms on the bunkhouse wing, while deep overhangs on the living room and kitchen roofs shade those spaces. Struts not only aid in support but give the shades the appearance of movable shutters.

Τhis area of Rhode Island

along Narragansett Bay was home to some of

America's most lavish country houses of the

19th century. Many were what would later be called

Shingle style, with a taut skin of shingles from head

to toe, complex massing, and a

more open plan, free from the

discrete spaces and ornate details

of earlier Victorian styles.

Property values and weather

have exacted a heavy toll on these

century-old mansions throughout New England and

the mid-Atlantic, but Rhode Island has been espe-

cially vigilant about preserving the best.

What gave even these huge houses their com-

fortable look is still sought after today. This modern-

The bunk wing appears to swivel away from public spaces.

Architect:
Jim Estes, AIA
Estes/Twombly Architects
Location:
Narragansett Bay, Rhode Island

A HANDSOME SLATE AND PEBBLE WALKWAY leads from the driveway to a welcoming, sheltered front porch with curved armrests, a pair of benches, and a view all the way through to Narragansett Bay.

COLOR, TEXTURE, AND MASS-ING make this coastal house fit perfectly into the land-scape. Roof and wall shingles imitate the texture and color of beach pebbles both above and below the tide line. The house is broken into several parts to make it less obtrusive.

73

day twist on the Shingle style possesses the rustic appearance of shingles, the fragmented massing—which can make a house look less imposing—and, of course, a free-flowing floor plan. The house borrows from other styles as well, including the overhanging eyebrows of the Stick style (earlier than the Shingle style) and the simplicity of vernacular Rhode Island farmhouses. What sets this house apart from the grand mansions of the gilded age is not only its size but also its deference to the landscape, preferring to step back rather than stand high on a cliff.

The site inspires not only the look of the house but also the layout, with public spaces spread out along the east, facing the bay. A separate two-story, four-bedroom section—the bunk wing—appears to swivel away from the public spaces to make more room and expand the view from the living room. The exuberant outside terraces and porches that were so celebrated in the Shingle-style mansions are apparent here from the front-door porch to the back, where a generous deck/porch wraps the waterside faces of the house.

THE KITCHEN/DINING ROOM shares a wide opening with the living space, separated by the stone fireplace. While the living room is a two-story space, the kitchen has a lower, cozier ceiling, which leaves room for a study above.

To lessen the perceived bulk of this wall-sized fireplace, a small, thin Pennsylvania stone was selected over the large glacier-rolled stones available locally. Oversized double-hung windows actually make the two-story space look more intimate.

In the dining room, a V-shaped wall of windows faces the water, giving a nautical look to the elevation from the outside and a focus for the view from inside.

The masonry wall not only separates spaces but brings them together with a fireplace on each side. The stone staircase is a heavy-duty version of a ship's ladder, leading to the study space over the kitchen.

Give and Take Revives a Connecticut Cape

Subtlety is not lost in this house. Delight is found around almost every corner: from the discovery of bright light doing a two-step with delicate lines of trim to the surprise of muntins making something inherently calm deliciously inviting.

DUO DICKINSON

WHERE A BREAKFAST ROOM HAD BEEN ADDED a few decades before, a hallway now connects the new, bigger kitchen with family room and dining room. A generous window seat also provides ample storage; cushions can be removed to make a mini greenhouse space.

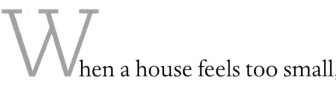

When a house feels too small,

the first impulse may be just to bump out the end wall or add another floor, but that rarely makes the best use of space or the best-looking house. What owners often crave beyond more rooms is more space in every room from entryway to kitchen to garage.

Sometimes it's easier to move or just start from scratch, but when a house is solidly built, with good lines and a great location, it's worth the effort to reconsider every inch in the quest for better livability. Each room in this graceful 1929 cape was evaluated for use, size, location, and relationship to other rooms and to lovely backyard gardens. The negatives were far-reaching: no mudroom, a cramped kitchen, a dark interior, minimal storage space, no master bathroom, little connection to the gardens, and not enough room for three teenagers.

The mudroom is a place lovely enough to linger in.

Architect:
Jennifer Huestis, AIA
Huestis Tucker Architects
Location:
Connecticut

IT'S IMPOSSIBLE TO TELL THAT THE BACK of this remodeled cape is entirely new. The curved roof is a new take on the old cape, as is the graceful brick chimney, but no matter, as proportions and materials blend perfectly. New walls don't match the original stone but are shingled to match existing dormer walls. New roofs match the old slate, an expensive choice but one that will last a century or more.

INSET DORMERS PRESENT AN UNDERSTATED PROFILE but are trickier to waterproof. These dormers, original to the 1920s cape, have stayed dry, a testament to excellent craftsmanship.

AN EXISTING SECOND FLOOR above this new breakfast room would have made for an 8-ft. ceiling, so the floor was dropped a foot below the existing level. That made space for heartier details, such as the half-height columns and elegantly trimmed arches. In the kitchen, windows win out over wall cabinets, and pantry space provides storage.

THIS COVERED BREEZEWAY was once the end of a poorly constructed family-room addition. Now it's put to much better use as an elegantly designed gateway to the lush backyard gardens.

A NEW MUDROOM TAKES ON A GLOW that raises its stature to sunroom. Each of the five family members has a wide closet and two drawers for storing outerwear and sports equipment. A bench offers room for changing footgear.

Spaces were transformed from top to bottom, some by changing use, others by changing size or orientation. A new garage turns 90 degrees to face away from the street and make room for another bay. Next to the garage, a slice of the house was cut out to make a stylish breezeway connecting the front to the gardens and the garage to the mudroom. The biggest design change—but least obvious from the street—enlarges the center of the house, pushing the kitchen toward the garden and making space for a generous breakfast room with fireplace. The lowliest of new spaces, the mudroom, was lined up along the inside wall of the new breezeway; now, it's a place lovely enough to linger in.

Shaping each room and detail was the desire to keep the house true to its style. Original walls are stone, but new exterior walls are finished with white cedar shingles that match those on existing dormers, a less expensive but compatible finish that makes the walls look original to the house. New finishes, details, and proportions interleave with the old finishes so well that the effect is seamless. That is, almost seamless, as the stone walls that were once outside were left uncovered, in part for the handsome texture but also as a quiet reminder of the old bones of a good house.

A MAJOR OVERHAUL to the center of the house provided the opportunity to slip in a second stairway that leads to the children's bedrooms. Now it's tough to be late to breakfast.

A Study in Contrast

Subtly and elegantly detailed, this quietly unassuming house makes a lot out of a little. The house and guest house are masterfully integrated with the surrounding landscape and pond.

JEREMIAH ECK

BUILT IN THE 1840S, this cottage was in such disrepair that the rear had to be rebuilt from the ground up. Finished with traditional shiplap siding, rear walls extend winglike past the volume of the interior space. A new stone wall, which trails into the pond on the other side, creeps out on this bank like the ruins of an old dam.

This house—two houses,

actually—and site are no overnight sensation. In fact, it took more than a century and a half of accretion and change to come up with this serene composition of building and landscape. Now the compound of the architect and his family, it began in several parts. First was the self-built cottage of an escaped slave constructed at the edge of a field; next to it came a church built in 1854 and converted to a house in the early 1900s.

Interior spaces are light and livable.

The family bought the church-turned-house and began renovating, but it wasn't until they had the good fortune to buy the field and cottage next door that the design became concrete and the construction went full bore.

Throughout the buildings and site, traditional elements and materials meet new, modern materials and detailing to make a composition that's often unpredictable and never heavy-handed. In the main house, existing double-hung windows were removed to make way for floor-to-ceiling

Architect:
Peter Bohlin, FAIA
Bohlin Cywinski Jackson
Location:
Waverly, Pennsylvania

WITH THE DOOR CLOSED, this renovated 1840s cottage looks true to its time, with shingles, wood trim, and divided-light windows. But when the door opens, there's a modern view straight through the house, into the garden and a man-made pond beyond. On this side, a handsome new field-stone wall extends the length of the compound.

IN THE MAIN HOUSE, new floor-to-ceiling window bays produce more light than the in-wall windows that once were here. In contrast to the age of the house, the opening is not cased but has a modern drywall return.

THIS BACK PORTION OF THE COTTAGE had collapsed and was rebuilt to follow the original roof line. Roof joists are left exposed. Rather than rebuild with the small, individual windows of the past, the architect opened the back wall by way of a modern, metal-framed window wall.

A SINK WITH A VIEW is important to any kitchen. This fixed metal-framed window provides a peaceful view of the wisteria arbor in the terrace between the main house and the dining addition.

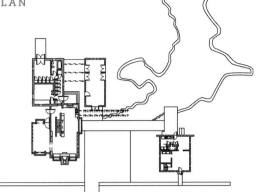

window boxes with modern narrow window frames and muntins. Where the cottage had deteriorated and was rebuilt, new exterior walls extend past the original house to make modern, planar wings. In contrast, to celebrate the age of the buildings, original timber posts and wide-board studs were exposed in the guest house, and floors in both houses were replaced with reclaimed heart pine. These contrasting elements aren't just eye candy for the architecturally savvy; details like these help give each house freshness, elegance, and even some humor.

Interior spaces are light and livable, but it's the spaces between and beyond the buildings that provide both comfort and delight. An intimate, wisteria-filled terrace between the main house and a new dining/project building offers a sheltered view of the fields. The all-new dining space and the guest cottage have an ever-changing view of a new pond. Because the view is to the north, the sun shines on the fields and pond from behind or to the east and west.

THE GUEST COTTAGE, built by a runaway slave, is laid bare to show the timber frame and wide-board wall studs. Plaster and lath were carefully stripped, leaving a ghostly texture that complements the patterns of chair fabric, radiator, and stair.

COMPLETELY MODERN IN BOTH PLACE-MENT AND DETAILING, this buffet shields the main-house dining-room table from passersby and from direct southern sun. Windows make up the remainder of the wall to allow in plenty of ambient light.

Two into One

A NEW TWO-STORY ATRIUM transforms the narrow townhouse acquisition into an expansive space with plenty of light and room to move or just to sit. Four palletlike steps twist their way up to a more conventional straight-run stair.

Outdoor space is hard to come by in the Capitol Hill section of Washington, D.C., so when long-time residents find a bit of greenery to buy, they go for it. When the owner of a 14-ft. by 44-ft. townhouse on a quiet mews got the opportunity to purchase the adjacent townhouse, he had no complaints about the smaller size of the house—11 ft. by 30 ft.—as it came with a small garden in the back. All the owner asked for were several vantage points from which to view his new garden; otherwise, the architect was free to experiment.

This combined house has plenty of light.

The old house was kept as is, with pale colors, exposed structure, and modern geometry, while the new house was largely gutted. A good chunk of the floor between the first and second floors was removed to make an atrium and a see-through set of stairs with open treads and metal pipe rails. Mechanical chases were built in corners against the front and back walls, and the side walls were left with exposed brick painted white. At certain places both upstairs and down, the bearing party wall between the houses was removed

Architect:
Mark McInturff, AIA
McInturff Architects
Location:
Washington, D.C.

IN THE JAM-PACKED CAPITOL HILL SECTION of Washington, D.C., any bit of greenery is welcome. The owner lived in townhouse #21 for years before he bought the townhouse next door and combined the spaces. These townhouses back up to larger, grander homes and enjoy the privacy of a mews.

WOOD IS USED LIBERALLY in the new addition, from the flat fir boards on the bedroom wall to the floorboards above, which are spaced slightly apart to create stripes of light. From the new master bedroom there's a view through the newly transparent wall to the tiny garden.

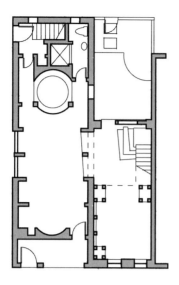

for access and, in the case of the dining-room balcony, simply for a view overlooking garden space. The back wall of the new space is now almost completely transparent, with commercial-grade metal windows, both fixed and operable. The sandblasted/glass door, a colored-glass window, frosted awning windows, and fir louvers gently shield both sun and view.

No longer two skinny townhouses with dark interiors, this combined house has plenty of light, a soothing view of a bit of green, and plenty of finely detailed wood and metal elements to delight the eye. As a bonus, the tall, dazzling two-story space is balanced by a new, sheltered master bedroom, making room for both jazz and coziness.

THE WHITE-PAINTED BRICK WALL was the party wall between the two townhouses. It was stripped of plaster and opened up to allow access and view between the existing house and the new. The owner, a part-time jazz musician, has space for two sets of drums—one in the existing living room and one under the new stair.

PUBLIC AND PRIVATE SPACES WORK TOGETHER to make an eminently livable house for one person, with a cozy, low-ceilinged bedroom tucked under the new upstairs sitting room. Canvas shades pull down to cover the closet and the bedroom door (this view shows the door shade retracted).

THIS VIEW IS FROM THE EXISTING LIVING ROOM, which retained its pale colors and exposed structure. The opening between the two houses is celebrated by beefy jambs and a broad wooden step up to a new stained concrete slab.

FLOOR HEIGHTS AND FINISHES VARY to indicate functions, with a raised, unstained fir platform in the new sitting room and stained wood-strip flooring in the kitchen/dining area.

A New Farmhouse
Takes Its Place in History

DOORWAYS IN THIS NEW FARMHOUSE are wider than those in older farmhouses, which allows for a more open plan. Elegant trim highlights each doorway and window to maintain the historic flavor.

This new house owes its appearance to the architects' careful study of its locale, a historic landmark town in the foothills of the Blue Ridge Mountains. It's not a slavish copy of a particular house but a tribute to the sense of the place, with sympathetic details, materials, and proportions.

Of these, proper proportion is the key to fitting into a historic fabric, but it's often disregarded. Here, proportion informs not only the house shape but also window placement and heft of details. The first-floor plan is almost square, like a traditional farmhouse, with some elements—the side screen porch, for example—looking as if they had been added on over the decades. Even from afar, the porches, the steeply sloped roof, the boxy gable ends, and the comparative height of the house give it a 19th-century

A large hearth room/kitchen is the focus of family life.

THIS NEW FARMHOUSE was so thoughtfully designed that it looks like a contemporary of its 19th-century neighbors. Fieldstone pillars, random-rubble foundation walls, a generous front porch, dog-house dormers, and a standing-seam metal roof are just a handful of the elements that add to the authenticity.

SOUTHERN PIEDMONT FARMHOUSES were painted with white lead in linseed oil, an inexpensive but hardy finish. Here, that same brilliant white is the color choice for clapboards and trim but is achieved with modern, nontoxic paint.

Architect:
Russell Versaci, AIA
Versaci and Neumann
Partners Architects
Location:
Blue Ridge Mountains, Virginia

CERTAINLY MORE UPTOWN than any farmhouse kitchen, this new kitchen is nevertheless just as inviting and comfortable. The cherry cabinets have simple, Quaker-style inset doors and drawers and are topped with oiled soapstone countertops at the perimeter and on the butcher block in the island.

LIKE THE EARLIEST FARMHOUSES, this hearth room focuses on a fireplace. The energy-efficient Rumford fireplace has a raised flagstone hearthstone that doubles as a bench and a picture-frame cherry trim. Exposed beams add to the virtual age of the space, along with period furniture and divided-light glazing.

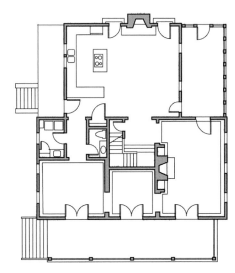

farmhouse look. Windows are symmetrically placed, and ample trim accents windows, eaves, porch entablature, and doors. Yet the trim is relatively simple, in keeping with a farmhouse.

Materials provide the next level of authenticity, from foundation to roof. The foundation is laid with local field-stone, exterior walls are bright white clapboard with trim painted the same white, and the metal roof, while copper, pays homage to the classic tin roof of the early farmhouse.

Inside, the farmhouse archetype of central stair hall dividing parlor from living/dining/kitchen space was reshaped for contemporary needs. The stair hall is turned sideways and enclosed with walls to allow living spaces to flow around it. A large hearth room/kitchen, which takes up the entire back half of the house, is the focus of family life—around the fireplace and cooking—as it was long before the American kitchen was hidden from public view.

ONE OF TWO MUCH-USED SIDE PORCHES, this one is designed to look not only added on, but filled even later with screened panels. To achieve this effect, the "exterior" wall is clad with clap-board and fit up with exterior windows like the rest of the house. The ceiling is painted bead-board, as on any honest porch.

DOGHOUSE DORMERS add space and light without having to raise the entire roof. These dormers are beautifully detailed, in keeping with the fine crafts-manship throughout the house.

Courting Quiet
with Geometric Harmony

THE HIPPED ROOF AND SLENDER, SYMMETRICAL WINDOWS on this Florida house recall the French Colonial style from the West Indies, but that's just the first impression. A closer look reveals modern restraint and a sculptural approach to detailing, with a grid overlaying the exterior and the asymmetrical placement of unadorned elements such as the chimney and garden walls.

THE MASTER-BEDROOM
BALCONY looks out on the
courtyard and the exact center
of the guest house and its
screen of palms. This axis is
one of several where elements
align to emphasize symmetry
and focus the view.

Living in town or in the suburbs

makes it easy to socialize, but it also makes it tougher to find

solitude. Imagine maintaining privacy with a golf course for

a backyard, a navigable waterway out front, and next-door

neighbors a glance away—a dream come true to

many but still a tricky design dilemma. This cool

jewel of a house near Vero Beach, Florida, takes

a cue from its tropical city cousins by focusing

the house around a courtyard while still present-

ing a polite face to the public.

A crisp modernism envelopes the traditional.

Sheltered by a single-story kitchen wing, a two-story main

house, a two-story guest house, and a tall garden wall, the court-

yard is an oasis of calm, with a streamlined pool taking up almost

half the space and tall palms providing shade and privacy. The

pool is just outside the living-room window, which fits between

walls with no trim, making the pool seem part of the living room.

While spaces have a luxurious feel, they are not grand in scale, so

Architect:
Hugh Newell Jacobsen, FAIA
Location:
Southern Florida

CURVED STEPS AND CRISP
CORNERS at this entry gate
exemplify the pristine
geometry that orders the
house, while vines growing
on the courtyard walls
soften the formal elements.

A DRAMATIC ADDITION TO THE LIVING SPACE, this switchback stair is more than a mere conveyance. Its glass rail and open treads all but disappear, giving it both emphasis and weightlessness.

VERTICALS AND GRIDS ALIGN AND ABUT in well-orchestrated harmony in this view of the courtyard and interior stair. A wood grid covers the joints of the cement-fiber paneling, an inexpensive but durable wall covering that doesn't mildew like wood.

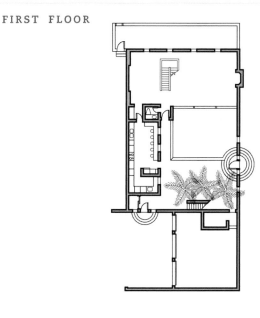

the house is comfortably intimate. Even the ubiquitous white finishes add serenity, not austerity.

The formal façade, facing the waterway, looks like a French Colonial house from the West Indies, with elongated, shuttered windows and a hipped roof with a shallow sweep. But there's a crisp modernism enveloping the traditional, with white everywhere, minimal trim, impeccable craftsmanship, and an emphasis on linear elements, such as the wood grid that overlays exterior walls. The elegant symmetrical façade that faces the waterway is the symbolic front, but the real entrance is through a gate around the corner. The secluded gate opens onto the courtyard, at once the most welcoming and most private of spaces.

THE SWIMMING POOL LAPS THE EDGE of the living room, and large windows minimize the separation. Because the view of the waterway is on the opposite side, the master-bedroom closets and bathroom are positioned on this side, but room was carved out for a balcony overlooking the pool.

THIS GARDEN WALL HAS A SIMPLE GRACE but its openings and proportions are carefully composed. A single window allows a partial view across to the neighbor but screens the pool from passersby.

Catch the Breeze, Renew the Spirit

SHADE IS A BLESSING in steamy-hot southern Louisiana, so locating the cabin in a grove of pines and hardwoods was a given. The adjacent meadow is both balm for overworked eyes and ball field for the family.

The dogtrot design makes the home roomy enough.

"Hot and humid" is the default

forecast for southeastern Louisiana for a good half of the year. This calls for zealous attention to certain design axioms: Orient the house to catch the breeze, offer plenty of shaded outdoor space, provide overhangs to keep out the sun, and allow windows to stay open in frequent summer rains. This design wisdom shapes the vernacular style called the dogtrot, a two-part house divided by a covered outdoor breezeway. The dogtrot arose from the difficulties of adding to a log house; instead, another house was built alongside the first, and the resulting breezeway was covered with a roof. A benefit of this configuration is that wind blowing through the breezeway increases airflow inside the house, assuming screen doors are open to the breezeway and windows are open elsewhere.

This contemporary version of the dogtrot, built outside Baton Rouge, hearkens to its predecessors in

Architect:
Stephen Atkinson, NCARB, AIA
Studio Atkinson
Location:
Southeast Louisiana

THE EXPANSIVE BREEZEWAY IS WELL LIT and welcoming, not to mention cool in the daytime. The owners enjoy walking through the covered outdoor space from living to sleeping areas. An outdoor fireplace adds warmth in cool months and ambience all year long.

A SIDE WINDOW GIVES a chapel-like look, with translucent corrugated siding outside and translucent plastic inside. Corrugated metal siding emphasizes the rural aspect of this dogtrot cabin, yet adds a cool sparkle both night and day.

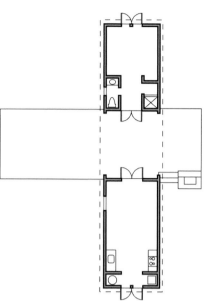

THE LARGER PART OF THE HOUSE contains kitchen, dining area, and sitting area. The wood floor continues to the door to extend the view but gives way to tile at the perimeter of the cabinets. Positioning utility closets at the south end helps buffer the sun from the kitchen.

intent and orientation, but its small size, symmetry, and artfully placed elements give it the spiritual aspect of a tiny chapel. In fact, the house design was inspired by an unbuilt design for a priest's retreat; now it's used by the architect's parents as a respite from their nearby city home. It's big enough for two, whether for overnight stays or an afternoon spent reading the Sunday Times, but the dogtrot design makes it roomy enough for a family gathering.

The smaller northern part is private, just big enough for a bed, bath, shower, and tiny closet, while the bigger south-facing portion contains a small sitting area and dining/kitchen space. Bigger even than the sum of those two parts is the generous deck that joins them and stretches beyond in both directions. A freestanding outdoor fireplace keeps heat from the house and extends the useful life of the deck into the cooler months. Even more generous is the field that this house watches over, plenty big enough for three-generation ball games.

FRENCH DOORS, PLACED ON EACH END and in the breezeway, align along the center axis. In warmer months, doors can be swung open and a roll-up screen employed. Corrugated metal doors, open in this photo, can close for security or weather protection.

THIS NORTH-FACING SLEEPING AREA is just big enough for a bed and a few small pieces of furniture.

In Response to the Climate

Duany Plater-Zyberk's innovative response to the tropical climate is an intricate, well-proportioned wood domicile housed within a simple, sturdy masonry envelope.

JOHN CONNELL

IT MAY BE SCORCHING HOT and sunny outside, but under the wide overhang of the roof this loggia makes a cool place to gather (this is a view from the bedroom balcony). Two of the house's four alcoves are visible here: The kitchen alcove is in the background, and the large living-room alcove faces the loggia.

Location isn't only the mantra

of real estate; it's the driving force behind the best house design. What makes this house ideal for coastal Florida would make it a disaster in the Rockies. The view may be spectacular in each place, but water and year-round warmth make this island house amenable to opening up to the outdoors. In fact, permanent outdoor spaces are woven among the enclosed rooms to make a variety of private/public and indoor/outdoor experiences. When it's time to sleep, the owners walk from the living room into the open-air loggia, peek at the stars, feel the breeze, and walk up steps to the bedroom. At lunchtime, they leave the studio, walk down a flight of breezeway stairs to the kitchen, and eat a sandwich on the loggia or—if it's blowing rain or dog-day hot—eat in the alcove off the kitchen.

Banks of windows add both intimacy and brightness.

Architect:
Duany Plater-Zyberk & Company
Location:
Coastal Florida

A STANDING-SEAM METAL ROOF in the fashion of vernacular Florida houses shelters this coastal island house like a colossal umbrella. The house is raised to allow any floodwaters to flow below living spaces. On this side of the house, which faces the bay, big square columns make a loggia for lounging and circulation.

THE LIVING ROOM AND ADJACENT ALCOVE complement each other with their distinctive qualities yet add up to make a larger, more varied space. Main ceilings are high, but alcove ceilings are much lower for a more intimate feel. This alcove is filled with operable windows for light and air, while the living room proper is solid.

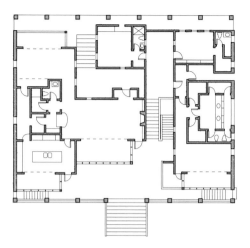

Inside, alcoves with lower ceilings and banks of windows add both intimacy and brightness to each major space.

But an island house comes with a price—occasional hurricanes and flooding. Accordingly, the two long side walls are built of concrete block to provide privacy and strength. The structure between is suspended from the side walls and raised an entire level above the ground to allow flood waters to pass between the block walls. Cars are parked under the house at ground level. On the waterside and streetside faces, large columns support a big hipped roof that shelters the interior spaces from sun and gentle rain. To resist storms, automatic metal shutters roll down between columns; the shutters also provide security when the owners are away.

WHEN A STORM IS FORECAST— or when owners are away for a long time—automatic metal shutters roll down between the columns to provide extra protection.

TO THE RIGHT OF THE STEPS, a partial wall supports the bedroom balcony, which is a few feet above the level of the decking of the loggia. This solid wall also screens occupants of the balcony, who can sit outside and watch the stars under the shelter of the roof.

WITH A CEILING MORE THAN 13 FT. HIGH, the kitchen has room for plenty of lighting, fans, and clerestory windows. The alcove just off the kitchen makes a more intimate space for coffee and the morning paper. Bright turquoise walls add to the tropical feel of the house.

THIS LIGHT-FILLED ALCOVE gets its glow from a bank of casement windows topped by fixed windows. Positioning the windows close to the ceiling magnifies the light as it bounces off the ceiling. The dining space itself has no direct windows but borrows all the light it needs from the alcove.

A Serene Retreat

Although completely new, this house already has an iconic quality that recalls the traditions of the Southwest. I especially like its one-room-deep plan, saddlebag porch, and thick walls that make it just as environmentally sympathetic as its ancestors.

JEREMIAH ECK

FROM AFAR, this house looks like a whitewashed church set gently on the prairie. Indeed, its historical precedent is the Sunday house, built throughout the region in the 19th century by immigrant German farmers.

The land and its history shaped this new house on the Texas prairie east of San Antonio. In the 1840s, German immigrants settled throughout the Hill Country of Texas, farming and building ranches and Sunday houses, intended for worship and socializing. Sunday houses were traditionally made of limestone, finished with stucco and whitewash, and shaped with a simple gable roof and a wood-framed lean-to porch, an essential in this dry, hot climate.

This ranch house, set in a natural, prairie-grass hollow by a pond and a grove of ancient live oaks, owes its appearance to the Sunday house but not its construction method. Limestone masonry is an expensive option today, so this house is actually built of doubled stud walls, set slightly apart to simulate the thickness of a solid stone wall. The stucco finish is hand-troweled and

A saddlebag porch stretches the full length of the house.

Architect:
Michael G. Imber, AIA
Michael G. Imber Architect
Location:
Hill Country, Texas

SALVAGED MESQUITE BARN LUMBER makes authentically aged lintels set deep in the stuccoed wall.

WALLS IN THE STAIR HALL are finished with wood boards that recall the wide plank walls built by early German-born farmers as quick, sturdy partitions. These are painted sage green, a reproduction color based on historic San Antonio houses. Red-brown Oklahoma flagstone imitates the packed-dirt floors of early German farmhouses.

THE ENTRYWAY FITS into a popped-out porch called a saddlebag, making it look like an addition to the original building. Windows are few to keep out the western sun, but the French doors set back under the overhang allow extra light into the house.

THE COOL, SERENE KITCHEN is finished with a combination of new and old, with stainless-steel hood and range, a glazed subway-tile backsplash, plain Shaker cabinets, and solid Spanish cedar counters. Throughout the house, main spaces are divided by plastered arched openings, which look as if they could be masonry.

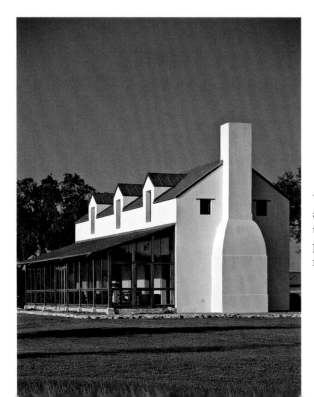

THE SCREENED SADDLEBAG PORCH not only multiplies the living and sleeping space but also softens the spare, white mass of the house. A series of lyrical spouts channel rainwater from the porch roof gutter, while the bulbous stucco chimney breast is a modern interpretation of vernacular farmhouse chimneys.

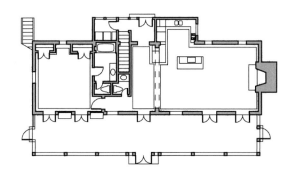

corners are gently rounded to give the house a look that's authentically old.

What confirms the historical look of the house is its long, thin shape. At 20 ft. wide—a single room across—and three times as long, its width is based on the relatively short span of the native live oak logs used to build the old Sunday houses. Unlike the northern farmhouse, which is square to make the most energy-efficient shape for cold weather, a long house has the added bonus of keeping the house cool with cross breezes. A porch with a lean-to roof, called a saddlebag porch in this region, stretches the full length of the house to catch the southeast breeze, shade the house, and provide a sleeping space.

But the house is no clone of Texas history. A closer look reveals details, proportions, and materials that are a shade more streamlined than the local vernacular. Roof meets wall with a taut, no-overhang connection, the chimney breast is a modern, oversized rendition of vernacular chimneys, and interior finishes include stainless steel and city-bred subway tiles. This spare, modern take on historic style suits the owner, a collector of 20th-century art.

AT 64 FT. LONG, this porch stretches the length of the house, serving not only as a sun shield but also as a major living space. The porch faces southeast to capture the prevailing Texas breezes. When the weather is right—much of the year—it becomes a sleeping porch, with Murphy beds that unfold from built-in cabinets.

Local Color Infuses
a Modern House

WHY THIS HOUSE

A tiny ensemble of spaces, this ebullient infill eliminates all distinction between inside and out—all while being thoroughly contained within its slot of space. Every detail is considered, every surface precisely defined.

DUO DICKINSON

THE COBALT BLUE OF THE DINING-ROOM WALL is a match for the brilliant Mexican sky and a balm for sun-baked eyes. Rich golden-yellow furniture and the mango-colored ceiling add contrast without sharpness. In the courtyard, a century-old pomegranate tree provides shade and beauty.

It takes a bit of daring to build

a house in another country—not to brave a foreign culture, but to leave behind the familiar and soak up the spirit of the new setting. This house in San Miguel de Allende, Mexico, was designed by architects from San Francisco, yet it embodies the local tradition of the town, a venerable 450-year-old community with many artists and crafts-people in residence. In fact, local arti-sans carried out much of the work, side by side with the architect-owners. The house reflects the colors, materials, shapes, and particulars of this high-altitude town and its brilliant blue skies and insistent heat.

Local construction techniques and available mate-rials steered the design to concrete posts and beams and salvaged bricks used for infill. Masonry received the customary painted plaster, and exposed concrete was hand

Tendrils of wrought iron wind next to thickset piers.

Architect:
House + House Architects
Location:
San Miguel de Allende, Mexico

THIS NEW 2,000-SQ.-FT. INFILL HOUSE replaces a tumble-down original with a modern house in sympathy with local design and crafts-manship. The heavy oak door leads to a much-used courtyard.

THE COURTYARD IS TRULY A RETREAT, both from baking sun and city life just beyond the oak door. The cobalt blue wall, studded throughout with frosted-glass light fix-tures, is plastered masonry, while the spiral stair and column are concrete.

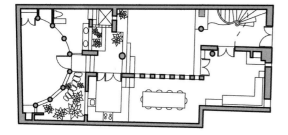

A TALL, NARROW WINDOW in this bathroom peeks out to a covered terrace above the courtyard, a private space for occupants of the upstairs bedrooms. Deep, rich tones of cobalt and mango balance coolness with warmth.

rubbed, then finished with lime wash, a durable, traditional finish that ages well and can be tinted with mineral pigments, such as the burgundy on the columns. The burgundy, along with rich cobalt, mango, and sage on plaster walls, suits the region's affinity for colors that stand up to the brilliant light. Locally made wrought iron is a prominent feature, as is indigenous stone: Slate was carted down mountains by donkey, and several shades of river rock make up the courtyard floor.

In response to both climate and city life, the courtyard style follows tradition. A courtyard is a social space that's shaded much of the day, and its configuration allows each room a window and view—even where houses are cheek to cheek. A courtyard allows interior doors to be transparent, as the courtyard itself is secured by a heavy oak door at the street.

Apart from function, these vernacular features create a house that's beautiful to live in, where elements pair to bring out the quintessence of each. Tendrils of wrought iron wind next to solid, thickset piers, and silky-smooth concrete abuts rough plaster. Delicate glass doors topped with transoms and sidelights provide transparency in contrast to the bulk of sheltering walls.

A CORNER OF THE LIVING ROOM IS BRIGHTENED by a sculpted masonry fireplace and a glass-block window with a glimpse of the street. The hearth, like all exposed concrete in the house, is hand polished and finished with pigmented lime wash. The delicate iron door frame was crafted by a local blacksmith.

THE HEFT OF ROUGH-PLASTERED MASONRY WALLS and posts and the lilt of curving wrought-iron railings and window frames make a lyrical pairing on this second-floor bedroom terrace level. The roof deck above is secured by another railing, this one completely wrought iron.

THE ROOFTOP SUNDECK above a second-floor bedroom has a view that skims rooftops—including the tiled roof of the owners' studio a few houses away—to the rugged hillside beyond. At 6,300 ft. above sea level, this region has abundant sunshine and brilliant blue skies much of the year.

Pueblo and Spanish Influences Shape a Hillside House

Adobe construction has a level of plasticity and solidity and allows for a miraculous manipulation of natural light in large and small ways. When adobe is set in contrast with wood and tile, as in this glowing and vibrant interior, a spare palette of materials reaps endless visual rewards.

DUO DICKINSON

A TRADITIONAL LAYER-ING OF BUILDING PARTS lends a handsome, serene look to the cool, comfortable living room. The major struc-tural elements are squared beams with carved corbels. On these are laid peeled logs called *vigas*, and spanning the vigas are *latillas*, which are rows of wood saplings laid in a herringbone pattern.

This Santa Fe house pays homage

to the traditional collective dwellings of the Pueblo Indian tribes of the Southwest, who built on steep mesas unsuitable for cultivation. Like a pueblo structure, in which many units are built adjacent to and above each other in stepping-stone formation, the spaces in this house are articulated separately but conjoined to make a more stable, weather-resistant whole.

Rooms unfold one by one.

While the ancient pueblo buildings had no windows and were accessed by ladders, the Spanish added windows, doors, and finely worked wood and metal details to the archetype. This house makes good and accurate use of these historic elements but within the context of a large house for modern living. Walls are built of adobe blocks, 2 ft. thick, but the blocks are improved by the addition of cement, which stabilizes the bricks and

Architect:
Michael Bauer, AIA
Bauer, Freeman, McDermott
Architects
Location:
Santa Fe, New Mexico

LIKE THE ANCIENT COLLECTIVE HOUSING TYPE, the pueblo, this Santa Fe house unfolds step-by-step down a hillside of piñon trees.

THE SERENITY AND BEAUTY of both adobe and indigenous wood are evident in this exterior view. The simplicity of the peeled post and rounded smoothness of adobe walls is complemented by the ornate corbeled column capital and delicate divided-light window.

RAIN ISN'T COMMON IN SANTA FE, but when it rains, it pours, so it's essential to have good drainage for flat roofs. This traditional Spanish detail, a *canale*, sits on a carved bracket support.

THREE STEPS UP FROM THE LIVING ROOM, the dining room sits in a small alcove with the kitchen beyond. All floors in the public spaces are glazed clay tile, which makes a cool floor in summer and a warm floor in winter.

A HEAVY BEAM SUPPORTED BY CARVED CORBELS frames the brightly lit window-seat alcove and imparts a sheltered feeling to the space. The fireplace in this master bedroom is a bee-hive *kiva* of traditional Pueblo design.

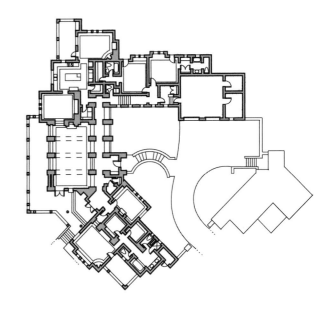

provides some water resistance. Inside, the wall finish is white gypsum plaster troweled smooth and rounded at the edges to duplicate the traditional finish of lime plaster. Traditional Pueblo/Spanish details include round-log *vigas*, square-cut beams supported by carved corbels, cool tile floors, and wrought-iron hardware.

The house provides an ever-changing view of the landscape, with rooms unfolding one by one as the house steps down the hill. Porches and covered walkways, called *portales,* extend from the dining room to the master bedroom and augment the family room and master bedroom. These provide both stunning views and shield the interior from the sun.

THIS LONG HALLWAY ACTS LIKE THE PORTALES that border the opposite side of the main rooms, providing a sun buffer and allowing for private or public circulation or gathering. *Bancos* fit under windows and between walls to provide space to sit. White gypsum plaster is troweled on smooth and rounded at the corners.

A Timeless Farmhouse

You might easily mistake this project for a farmhouse from the past, and that's its real appeal. By keeping it simple, the architect has given us a timeless house, one that will keep its fascination for years to come.

JEREMIAH ECK

LIKE ANY HONEST FARMHOUSE, this new version sits on the crown of a knoll next to a grove of sheltering trees, with the garage nestled down the hill. A green gable roof, symmetrically placed windows, and a broad porch establish the look of a traditional farmhouse.

The sight of an old farmhouse

on a hillside brings out the bucolic in most of us, and it offered just the right inspiration for this rural Minnesota house. Ideally sited beside a grove of sheltering trees, the house shields its west and south faces with a broad, shady porch, that most evocative of farmhouse motifs. The breadth of the porch—wrapped around two sides and projecting past a third—is what gives this house the grace and utility of its forebears, along with double-hung windows, white clapboards, and a steep (12-in-12) green-shingled gable roof.

Rooms are less self-contained than in a classic farmhouse.

Inside, the plan draws on the classic farmhouse layout of four rooms—parlor, living room, dining room, and kitchen—with a mudroom and porch attached. Traditional farm living required the porch and mudroom as a transition from field to floor, and today's families wish for the same convenience. In this house, there's no

Architect:
Jean Rehkamp Larson, AIA,
with Steve Mooney
SALA Architects
Location:
Chaska, Minnesota

IT'S EASY TO JUSTIFY SPACE for a generous center hall, even upstairs. This hall allows ample room to circulate and space to be still and read, play, or talk. A projecting linen closet buffers separate bedroom entrances.

A SCRIM OF FLOOR-TO-CEILING SCREENS is supported by white-painted 2x4s, transforming the wraparound porch to the most useful—and good-looking—appendage a living room can have.

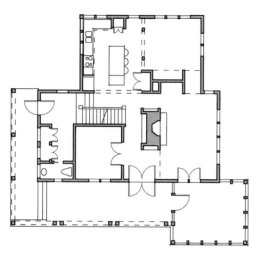

TWO WIDE HALLWAYS guide circulation and light from space to space. This hall runs from the front porch to the kitchen, where a window defines the end of the axis. The bookcase at right, which backs up to the living room fireplace, faces the stair to make a handy spot for browsing.

formal entrance for guests—everyone enters the mudroom through the north side near the garage.

In keeping with today's more informal living, rooms are less self-contained than in a classic farmhouse—especially the dining room and kitchen, which are separated only by half walls, columns, and lattice. The traditional living room was enlarged and opened to the hall, and the parlor was transformed into a more private "away room" that can take on the role of den, studio, media center, or guest bedroom.

This house is filled with light, due to fewer walls and larger, more abundant windows than you'd find in a traditional farmhouse. Doors are also glazed to bring in light year-round, but divided lights and time-honored proportions maintain that century-old farmhouse look.

EACH MAJOR SPACE in this up-to-date farmhouse is defined, but not closed off, as it would be in an older home. Low walls, columns, and lattice delineate where the dining room ends and the kitchen begins, yet it's easy to talk, see, and move between the two spaces.

THE LIVING ROOM is neither a dimly lit, stiffly furnished farmhouse parlor nor a rough-and-tumble modern family room. Instead, it's a comfortable space for guests and family alike to enjoy each other's company. Across the wide hall, an away room can provide either sanctuary or a place to play music without disturbing inhabitants of the living room.

Small in Footprint
but Tall in Stature

WHY THIS HOUSE

In a daring play with scale and convention, this design for a getaway home provides the owners with a refreshing, toy-like alternative to their everyday domicile.

JOHN CONNELL

THE DINING SPACE IS KEPT INTIMATE by the lowered ceiling above, and the wood finish mirrors the flooring to give the space richness. A slate tile strip acts as both hearth and visual divider between living and dining areas. Light from the loft above and screened porch below add volumes to this small house.

A house built for weekend living

is often smaller and more informal than its weekday counterpart, so why is it often a more comfortable and striking design? The weekend house requires spaces and surfaces to do double duty, privacy is sometimes at a premium, and finishes are not as elegant. What it has to its advantage, however, is a focus on the landscape, as the weekend house is usually a place to retreat from the town or city and to enjoy the natural surroundings. In addition, the weekend house offers a sense of well-being, not just because it's time to relax but because rooms are often more intimate—a windfall of having to make less space cover more ground.

A screened porch is a boon in the land of the blackfly.

This 1,200-sq.-ft. weekend house on Washington Island in Wisconsin derives its design from the classic farmstead, with its individual buildings amassed over time in response to specific needs. Three individual parts make up the whole: a cottage with

THREE INDIVIDUAL SHAPES make up this small weekend cabin in Wisconsin. A tall, gabled form with shed attachments front and back holds dining and living spaces, the kitchen, and a screened porch. A smaller, single-gabled cottage contains two bedrooms, and a silo encloses two bathrooms. A short covered walk connects the living cottage with the sleeping quarters. Shingles blend with the woods, while white trim and red metal roofs evoke Wisconsin farm buildings.

Architect:
Frederick Phillips, FAIA
Frederick Phillips & Associates
Location:
Washington Island, Wisconsin

At 14 ft., the living room is not wide, but it's plenty big enough for friendly conversation among family and guests who sit on the couches or the long window seat. The high ceiling adds loft to the spare space, and wood wainscoting and trim add depth and warmth.

While the bathrooms in the silo have no windows, the hallways between the silo and sleeping cottage are glazed to provide plenty of light.

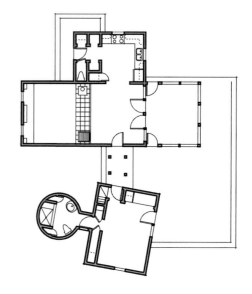

living and dining spaces and a kitchen, a sleeping cottage with two bedrooms, and a silo with two bathrooms. To go from the living cottage to the bedroom space requires a brief exposure to the weather, but the payoff is a spectacular view of the lake. Because this is a year-round haven, it was also essential to create sheltered space from which to enjoy the view at leisure. There are two such spaces: a deck that is partly covered and a screened porch—a boon in the land of the blackfly.

Dividing the house into separate chunks hasn't made the spaces seem cramped; in fact, the clever use of vertical space makes living and dining spaces both cozy and airy. The dining space is covered by the loft to make dining more intimate. Even though dining and living spaces have the same-sized footprint, the living room looks bigger because it shares light and space with the loft, and its ceiling is high and sloped. This attention to making the most out of a little space and simple materials makes the house equal to its exceptional setting.

THE SLEEPING COTTAGE CONNECTS TO THE LIVING COTTAGE by a covered link, allowing a dramatic view of the lake when approaching the house and also making a protected spot outdoors to pull up a chair to view the sunset. The owners are always aware of the landscape as they move between the two main parts of the house.

Townhouse Transformation

In this beautifully recycled home, Morgante-Wilson's varied column treatments highlight the role of history both playfully and effectively.

JOHN CONNELL

INTERIOR WALLS WERE REPLACED with a steel structure, which greatly increased the amount of light and the depth of field. Yet these same beams and columns serve to separate the dining space from the living space. Colors are kept neutral to maintain serenity.

S tately and solid,

the streetside façade of this Chicago townhouse offers no hint of its contemporary, sunshot interior, now completely transformed to make it more livable for a young family. Built in the 1880s as two apartments and later split into three, the house fills most of the 25-ft.-wide lot, so interiors were dimly lit by just front and rear windows. Yet the owners wanted to double the size by making a three-story addition in the rear, with the potential of further limiting access to daylight.

Details, finishes, and furniture contrast, but gently.

But adversity became the mother of invention: The architects recommended gutting the house except for the front and side walls and rebuilding the interior with a steel structure to allow for fewer walls and more light. A critical element of the design was to open the roof to make a large skylight over a new central stairway.

This big switchback stairway has become the focus of the renovated house, and it acts as an atrium that guides both traffic and light. Now spaces flow into each other to dramatically increase

Architect:
Morgante-Wilson Architects
Location:
Chicago, Illinois

IN CONTRAST TO THE FORMAL, BRICK-AND-SANDSTONE FACE of this Chicago townhouse, the back of the building breaks loose with a medley of traditional materials in an untraditional composition.

THE KITCHEN IS THREE STEPS UP from the breakfast room and family room, but a pass-through provides an easy way to get food to the table.

To visually lighten the upper cabinets that face the breakfast room, doors are glazed and an open grid of shelving makes an airy, transparent buffer. The floor adds a subtle punch to the space with its contrasting panels of light, zebra-striped hardwood, and wider, dark-stained wood.

As part of the new addition to the house, the master bedroom enjoys the luxury of a variety of ceiling heights. Splitting the chimney flues, which makes a bold statement on the rear façade of the house, allows room for a small but cheery window above the mantel.

The subtle but exciting contrast of geometry, color, and texture continues outside the townhouse, with a collage of lattice, brick, siding, fencing, and stone. Greenery softens the space, turning it into a peaceful oasis in the city.

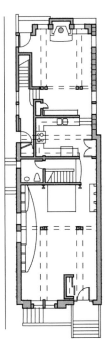

light and livability for a growing family, yet individual rooms are kept distinct and at a comfortable scale by the orderly layout of exposed, white-painted steel beams and Victorian-style steel columns.

Hand in hand with the use of light and space, attention to detail is key to why this house delights. Details, finishes, and furniture were selected to contrast, but gently. Structural elements, which could look stolid, become light and graceful with the addition of white paint. Horizontal surfaces from floor to countertops and ascending linear elements such as stair rails are dark, which adds elegance, vigor, and drama. Contrasting or not, colors are kept neutral, allowing the most important elements in the house—the family—to add personal touches and to enjoy the light and space that make the house so easy to live in.

THIS THREE-STORY SWITCHBACK STAIR is the soul of the renovated townhouse. By way of a large skylight and clerestory windows on each floor, the stairway brings light to all interior spaces during the day, and recessed and decorative lighting add drama and brilliance by night. The dark-stained wood handrail and copper-tubing railing below give energy and direction to the light stairway.

A Clear Field of Vision

Simple doesn't have to mean boring or predictable; here, it stands for elegance and clear-headedness. The side benefit of this simplicity is that the house sits gracefully in the landscape, defining a part of it completely while at the same time deferring to its grandeur.

DUO DICKINSON

AN APPRECIATION FOR THE CRISP, TAUT AESTHETIC of Shaker design influenced the choice of prestained gray cedar clapboards and tongue-and-groove siding, as well as the galvanized-steel standing-seam roof, which overhangs to make a sharp shadow. Abundant windows—a given with this view—lend the house transparency and lightness.

There's often a stark beauty

about buildings built for service, whether for farm or factory. Utility demands a spare shape and functional materials, yet these very elements can be ornament enough. The Shakers crafted buildings in the name of utility but with underlying grace and loveliness that still inspire us today. This house complex on a 10-acre site in northwest Indiana was influenced by that Shaker aesthetic, along with local farm vernacular and the work of artist Donald Judd, whose spare sculptures and buildings stand in the grasslands of west Texas.

Like a farmhouse, this house is set on a crest overlooking a meadow and sheltered on the backside by woods. On clear days, the Indiana Dunes and Lake Michigan are visible to the north. Laid out both for privacy and community, the house is arranged in parts around a courtyard. A two-story high wing contains living room, library, two bedrooms, and two baths. Attached at a right angle, but only one story high, is a service

Banks of windows add intimacy and brightness.

Architect:
**Dan Wheeler, AIA,
Wheeler Kearns Architects**
Location:
Northwestern Indiana

SET ON A KNOLL overlooking a 10-acre meadow, this Indiana house takes its shape and aesthetic from several sources, notably Shaker design, the local farm-building vernacular, and the spare aesthetic of sculptor Donald Judd. A workshop wing encloses a courtyard to the left of the two-story main house.

A WALL OF FRENCH DOORS AND WINDOWS, a glass and clear plastic table, and light, softly rubbed concrete floors make an elegant contrast with dark stained chairs and cabinet and with the warm, less formal kitchen beyond.

129

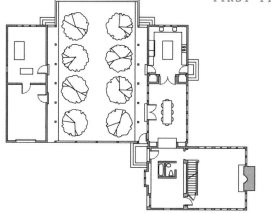

DISPLAYED OBJECTS PROVIDE TEXTURE and color in contrast to the pale concrete and white-painted woodwork. Collections of vessels are elegantly displayed on delicate glass shelves in the dining room and burly wood shelves at the entrance to the library.

wing with kitchen and dining room. A twin service building with workshop and storage stands across the courtyard. The vernacular spirit of farm buildings—more barn than farmhouse—is recalled in the finishes, from gray-stained siding to galvanized-steel standing-seam roofs. A ready supply and low price determined the choice of cleft-faced Indiana limestone on the courtyard and front steps.

Overlaying the physical references to Shaker and barn buildings is a sophisticated play of transparency and opaqueness, a reference to Donald Judd's barracks-turned-gallery buildings in which bands of windows wrap tops of solid walls. Almost half of the two-story wing is filled with windows; because it faces north and the only onlookers are coyotes and turkeys, there's no need for curtains, only for sheer rollup shades tucked at the top of each window. Interior spaces reflect the same balance of open and closed, symmetrical and informal found on the outside. Generous displays of objects are in friendly competition with the view outside, a perfect example of the poise between the landscape and the artifact.

MASTER BEDROOM WALLS are filled with windows, as the view stretches to Lake Michigan on clear days. Bottom sash are fixed while upper casements are open to breeze and view, and an unobtrusive sheer rollup shade is at the ready at each window head.

THE WARM, HIGHLY FIGURED CHARACTER of wood cabinetry sets off the crisp coolness of concrete floors, aluminum chairs, and stainless-steel appliances. Radiant heat adds even more comfort to the silky-soft concrete.

ALL WINGS OF THE HOUSE are finished in the same manner, but the two-story portion receives the most attention due to its height, its more complex window composition, and a tall, galvanized smokestack anchoring the end.

A New House with an Ageless Soul

By nature, homes are the combination of line, plane, space, and shape. These abstract concepts become divinely domestic when they weave together human-friendly spaces, careful crafting, and the flow of light and spirit that evidence a gifted designer's intimate touch.

DUO DICKINSON

OBSCURE GLASS ALLOWS IN LIGHT but blocks views of neighboring houses, a mere few feet away on each side. This design trick is used throughout the house to make the best use of reflected light—better than the usual configuration of locating windows a foot below the ceiling.

There's often more to weaving

a new house into the fabric of an established neighborhood than

meets the eye. Polite, but not to a fault, this Minneapolis house

fits into its 1920s neighborhood by a respect

for existing proportions, colors, and setbacks.

The most obvious aspect of the design is that

there's no two-car garage plopped down

beside or in front of the house. That's thanks to a mews, the alley

in the center of the block where garages are built and garbage is

collected. Any neighborhood lucky enough to have a mews is

likely to have an attractive street face.

Light plays a major role.

Fitting in doesn't mean being a copycat; in fact, it's easy to

incorporate contemporary detailing if at least massing and color

are sympathetic. This house has the deep overhangs, shallow

roof slope, brick base, and basic square shape of its neighbors,

and the cream and soft green colors suit. Horizontal trim and

ribbons of windows help put the house square in the Prairie style,

Architect:
Sarah Susanka, AIA, with Paul Hannan
Location:
Minneapolis, Minnesota

DEEP OVERHANGS, A BRICK FOUNDATION, grouped windows, and a square shape tie the house to its neighbors—as does the lack of a front-facing garage. This house fits into its neighborhood so successfully that passersby stopped during finish work to ask when the remodeling had begun.

A RECESSED ENTRY ALONG-SIDE THE HOME OFFICE bids a weatherproof welcome without adding to the bulk of a front porch. But finding the front door isn't hard because a projecting roof signals the entry.

TWO LOUVERED SCREENS FLANK the dining room to share light and glimpses between spaces. Flat trim makes a subtle but well-dressed frame for openings; this detail not only helps make clear transitions between rooms but also unifies the house.

IMAGINE THIS SPACE with a simple, flat 8-ft. ceiling, and much of the ambience is gone. The ceiling is just over 8 ft., but it seems higher because of the encircling soffit and the change in wall color from darker to lighter.

SPACE IS SHAPED to give each room a quality of containment and a sense of connection to other spaces. The opening beside the range allows the countertop to serve the dining room beyond, but it also makes each space seem larger. Light-toned trim, cabinetry, and flooring have a serene look, but a few darker-toned wood elements—the pantry door and trim over the fireplace—add a bit of spice.

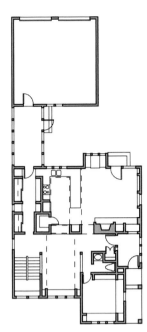

indigenous to the Midwest. The deeply recessed entry was rare in the 1920s, but a projecting roof clearly reads "here's the front door," and the covered porch makes a most welcome transition in snow or rain.

Inside, finishes are more contemporary and spaces are more open than in a 1920s house, but certain time-tested designs define space. Halls and door openings are framed with headers and jambs—rather than simple drywall—to make definite transitions, and windowlike openings in interior walls help tie spaces together. Light plays a major role, with clusters of windows in most rooms and single windows positioned to illumine dark spots or to catch the eye, such as at the end of a hall. Repeatedly, ceiling heights change to signal a change in function or to reinforce either intimacy or community. A line of flat trim running throughout the house serves as a median between changes in wall color and changes in ceiling height.

A SOFFIT IS HANDY for concealing mechanical ductwork and plumbing, but it's just as useful for defining space. The soffit that circumscribes this great room adds coziness to the eating alcove and defines the edge of the kitchen.

Cube with a View

Exposed structure and window walls make up the visual language of this contemporary icon. Perched delicately on a gentle slope at the edge of a meadow, the transparent house still holds its own three decades after completion.

JEREMIAH ECK

THIS FIRST-LEVEL LIVING AREA IS OPEN the full height of the 25-ft. cube, adding drama and loft to the space. The spiral stair climbs to the second-level sleeping/sitting area, from which a ladder accesses the topmost sleeping area.

Glass is not the wall material

that immediately comes to mind when conjuring the image of a cabin. All-glass houses have startled neighbors on rare occasions for a half-century or so, but a cabin—by definition small and isolated—actually makes sense as a transparent object. Set on a 40-acre site in Wisconsin that's part meadow, part forest, this glass cube was built 30 years ago by noted architect Ralph Rapson and his wife Mary, and they've been coming here to get away ever since, making only the smallest cosmetic changes to the house over the years. Today's renewed interest in modern design and the accompanying emphasis on transparency and exposed structure make the house fit in with the 21st century as well as the last.

Views are framed by the many structural elements.

The structure is composed of two layers, each intent on making the house both transparent and strong. Window walls form the first layer, with stock casement and fixed windows and sliding glass doors stacked in three rows and held in place by a wood post-and-beam frame. The windows are clad with white

Architect:
Ralph Rapson, FAIA
Ralph Rapson and Associates
Location:
Wisconsin

THE WINDOW WALL is made up of stacked and butted stock casement and fixed windows, plus a few sliding glass doors, all fit within a post-and-beam frame. This white window wall is braced by a black-painted wood exoskeleton for strength and flexibility.

TUCKED LIGHTLY AMONG A GROVE OF TREES, the glass cube cabin overlooks a river and valley beyond, the source of views both peaceful and wild. The two upper levels stay clear of the cube's perimeter to add transparency and buoyancy to the appearance.

COLORS, TEXTURES, MATERIALS, AND SHAPES mix in an interior composition that is at once artful and cheerful. Structural and mechanical elements are black or white, and diagonal boards are on both floor and walls. The hatch in the kitchen floor accesses a mechanical space.

WOOD DECKING ON THE FIRST LEVEL is laid at an angle and cut into platforms that appear to float in crushed white marble.

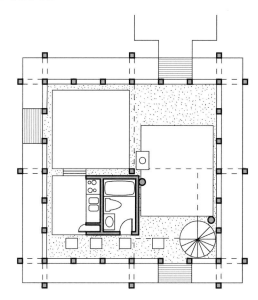

aluminum, and the wood is painted white to give the skin a light, clean look. For strength and flexibility, the window wall is braced by a wood exoskeleton with adjustable tie rods; that frame is painted black to look like steel and be less assertive. To maintain buoyancy, the top two levels end shy of the window wall, and the first-floor wood decking floats gently on a sea of crushed white marble. Only the bathroom is distinguished by solid walls, which help define spaces on the first level.

A forest borders the north, but to the east, south, and west, the glass cabin is open to distant views across a river valley, save for a few trees planted close by. Sunsets and sunrises are on display, along with the dance of fireflies and the fury of lightning storms and blizzards. From the inside, views are framed by the many structural elements in an ever-changing panorama. And best of all, the owners recently bought the neighboring 40 acres, so the view should last a good long while.

THE TOP-LEVEL SLEEPING AREA, accessible by a ladder from the second floor, is at once private and completely open to the view of landscape and weather.

Canadian Boathouse

IT APPEARS TO FLOAT, but this boathouse/cabin is rock solid, supported by a timber frame that's attached to submerged rock-filled cribs resting on a granite ledge. Multi-layered, perpendicular panels of wood boards make a complex but subtle skin. Gray, greens, and natural woods reflect the colors of the landscape.

This is no mere house overlooking

the water—it is *in* the water: part boathouse, part house for living. Built in and over Muskoka Lake, Ontario, this captivating structure lodges two boats indoors and one outdoors. Above, and accessible by an outside staircase, is a sleeping cabin complete with kitchenette, shower and bath, sitting room, and several outdoor spaces, including a covered porch, a deck, and a roof garden. There's a larger house up the hill, but that's for guests; this is the owner's retreat. A broad wood deck and a stone wall bounding the grounded end of the house provide plenty of space for guests and owners alike to gather and slough off the stress of the workweek.

Wood gives the boathouse the sophistication of a yacht.

But simple needs and a modest size belie the complexity of detail, patterns, and space found in this house. Among the precedents for the house are the Adirondack

Architect:
Brigitte Shim and Howard Sutcliffe
Shim-Sutcliffe Architects
Location:
Muskoka Lake, Ontario

WITH DOORS TO THE BOAT SLIPS OPEN, deck sitters can see not only past but also through the house itself. There's a mini kitchen at left for family and guests, but the second-level living space with terrace is the private domain of the owners.

RARELY IS A BATHROOM GRACED with such attention to detail, such fine craftsmanship, and such a view. Windows, countertop, and cabinets are mahogany with a soft, rubbed finish. Green cabinet doors and a black kickspace and undercounter recess make the mahogany look even richer.

ALMOST ALL INTERIOR SURFACES are finished with wood—primarily mahogany—as it's more forgiving of movement than drywall or plaster. Kitchenette cabinet doors are the same green as bathroom doors but a different style. This view from the entrance extends to the lake.

THE CURVED CEILING OF DOUGLAS FIR STRIPS gives the bedroom/sitting room the elegance of a yacht and creates both shelter and spaciousness. It's a four-season space, with big operable windows for summer breezes and a fireplace to ward off the chill. Outside, the deck's low wall and slender raised railing provide both safety and a long view.

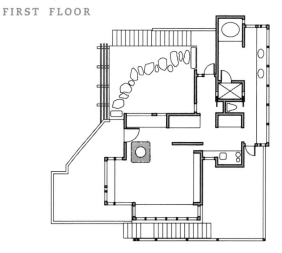

camps of upstate New York, local log cabins and Victorian cottages, Japanese architecture, and fine wooden boat craftsmanship. The vernacular is tempered by a modernist hand, with clean lines such as flush cabinets with stream-lined hardware and exposed structural elements. While the living spaces are conjoined, panels, angles, and distance keep functions discrete but not confined.

Most finishes are wood, as the timber-frame-on-sunken-cribs structure is prone to movement, and wood is more forgiving than plaster or drywall. The predominance of wood results in an interior filled with beautifully crafted surfaces from floor to ceiling and gives the boathouse the sophistication and tautness of a yacht. With colors that reflect the surroundings, and windows and decks positioned for view and breeze, this boathouse is perfectly attuned to its surroundings. It does everything but set sail.

NO ELEMENT IS LEFT UNCONSIDERED. Brilliant rectangles of sky are visible in the open porch roof to allow dappled light into the bathroom. The light fixture is made from a large Mason jar and metal ellipses coated with fly fisherman's phosphorescent paint; at night the fixture looks like moths fluttering around a lightbulb.

THE ZENLIKE WHIRLPOOL SPACE is completely finished with wood—marine plywood walls, Douglas fir strips on the curved ceiling, and a mahogany duck board grating over the floor drain. A slender window at right lets in a lake view.

Wright-Inspired Ranch

PARTITIONS RATHER THAN FULL-HEIGHT WALLS provide privacy for the library and master bedroom beyond yet allow light and views to flow. Concrete floors in this great room, in the entryway at left, and in the bathrooms are cast with radiant heat systems, a gentle warmth that's not only a comfort to cold feet but does away with radiators and registers.

Consider the stick-built

19th-century house: rectangular walls with framed openings, flat ceilings under or between rafters, defined rooms with doors, discrete windows, and a tidy plan. Now consider what a radical change the 20th century brought to house design, spurred by the Arts and Crafts movement's refusal to build on historical precedent. The Prairie style emerged from this sea change, with Frank Lloyd Wright at the helm. Features of the Prairie style focus on the horizontal, such as low-pitched roofs with deep overhangs, bands of windows, and soffits and partial walls that shape internal space. Although the first Prairie-style houses were two-story, Wright and others applied the same principles to the one-story ranch house design.

Deep overhangs give the house a substantial look.

This new house in Wisconsin—home to some of the earliest Prairie-style houses—owes its allegiance to Wright's design philosophy, such as the low, overhanging

Architect:
Ken Dahlin, AIA
Genesis Architecture
Location:
Wisconsin

WINDOW HEADERS ARE HIDDEN above the ceiling, so this roof appears to float above the window walls with no support. The lack of corner mullions adds to the illusion.

THE GREAT ROOM is three steps down from the rest of the house, creating a higher ceiling (and steps for sitting during parties or for grandkids anytime). The lowered ceiling and the fireplace masonry mass provide an intimate space for a hallway art gallery.

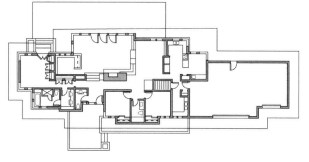

A HALLMARK OF THE RANCH VERSION of the Prairie style is a recessed entryway protected by a deep overhang, in contrast to a traditional porch entry. This entry is transparent, allowing a view through the great room to the woods. The tall Wright-inspired etched-glass window illumines and screens a powder room.

THE TRADEMARK LOW-SLOPE, deeply overhanging roof of the Prairie style helps keep snow, water, and staining at a minimum without the need for gutters, and it shields the house from summer sun while allowing in the lower winter sun. At night, interior lights shine on smooth exterior soffits to make a soft glow that's visible inside, so windows don't look like dark holes.

roof and his later Modern emphasis that interior space express itself on the exterior and that spaces flow within the house. Applying these elements to the ranch style is ideal for the owners of this house, a retired couple who prefer the ease of one main level, with a great room that's just a few steps down. Large windows, some with no corner mullions, bring the outside (a nature preserve) as close to the interior as possible, and deep overhangs maintain energy efficiency and give the house a substantial sheltered look while keeping the scale in sync with the flat terrain.

Unlike the rectangular plan of a simple traditional house, here, each interior space is expressed by a change in the perimeter wall. Yet the horizontal banding of brick, windows, and wood trim ties the shifting wall planes together. Inside, light and view flow among rooms to expand the perceived size and make use of natural light. Where privacy is important, tops of partition walls are glazed to block sound. Craftsmanship, another important tenet of the Prairie style, is evident from ceiling to floor, with regimented masonry, perfectly matched cabinet faces, and velvety smooth concrete.

CORNER WINDOWS AREN'T GLASS but a strong, transparent, energy-efficient acrylic, which can be easily butt-joined to make the windows dissolve and the kitchen seem open to the outdoors. To take full advantage of the view, kitchen storage is handled in generous base cabinets and a pantry rather than in upper cabinets.

VARIED CEILING LEVELS and layered wall planes sculpt space that's both intimate and expansive, depending on the point of view. Muted colors—shades of brown, cream, and gray—add to the subtle complexity.

Riverside, Shingle Style

WHY THIS HOUSE

Unpretentious, friendly, and embracing, this house of open interiors and careful exterior expression is the embodiment of comfort.

DUO DICKINSON

THE ST. CROIX RIVER IS THE FOCAL POINT of the kitchen/eating space, and the ceiling is raised over the eating area to make the most of that view and the ambient light. Throughout the house, finishes on trim and other wood elements make a subtle and sophisticated contrast of dark and light.

BROAD, STEEPLY SLOPED
FRONT-FACING GABLES are
the highlight of this modern-
day version of a Shingle-style
house in Minnesota. The
projecting gables provide
symbolic and physical shelter.

Water—whether ocean,

river, lake, or pond—has always been an enticement for

anyone looking to build a home. We love water for its

recreational promise, for its attraction to wildlife, and for

its ever-changing appearance. One way to balance the wild,

sometimes unpredictable nature of

water is to design a house that looks

as if it can stand the test of time and

weather. That's the appeal of the

Shingle-style house, born in the late

19th century as a seaside shingle-coated

Nooks and crannies make comfortable spaces.

version of the Queen Anne style and much admired for its

sheltering, sprawling, and imminently comfortable and

permanent image. It's the inspiration for this family-

friendly house overlooking the St. Croix River.

Elements of the Shingle-style house abound here,

from the shingled walls with no corner boards to the wide,

overhanging front-facing gables to the eyebrow-shaped

THE VIEW FROM THE MASTER
BEDROOM is almost like that
from an old-fashioned river-
boat, with a horizontal deck
railing and wood decking.
The eyebrow-shaped roof
and opening recalls Shingle-
style precedents.

Architect:
Michaela Mahady, AIA, and Dan Porter
SALA Architects
Location:
on St. Croix River, Minnesota

149

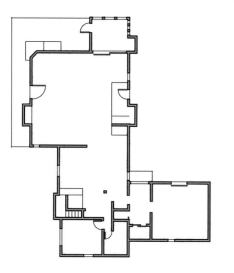

balcony outside the master bedroom. Inside, spaces and details are more contemporary and casual than a Shingle-style house from a century ago. Woods are brighter, windows are more abundant, and the exposed structure is highlighted with modern detailing such as metal banding.

But the intent—comfortable family living—remains the same from generation to generation. Here, rooms are both plentiful and generous so that parents and kids can have their own spaces, but those spaces are close enough or open enough so that kids and parents aren't far apart. A variety of nooks and crannies make comfortable spaces for quieter activities.

THE MOST VALUABLE REAL ESTATE in a house is often a built-in bench, whether in a kitchen, bedroom, or, less commonly, dining room, as it is here. Built-in storage beneath the seat makes the space especially functional.

PROVIDING MORE THAN MERE CIRCULA-TION SPACE, this hallway takes its castlelike character from gabled ceilings and well-positioned lighting. It's wide enough to accommodate kids' play spilling out of bedrooms.

THE LIVING ROOM IS A STEP DOWN from the entryway and the open kitchen so that its space is defined but not separate. A stone fireplace, an exposed post-and-beam structure, and rustic furniture make for a cozy family retreat.

UPSTAIRS AND DOWN ARE CONNECTED by a stair designed with wide landings and ample storage for toys and books, making great places for kids to relax, read, and play.

Style and Delight on a Budget

A simple but provocative move transforms a basic cottage into a constellation of opportunities and surprises. Inspired by Rockhill's playful use of materials and dedication to sustainable design, this modest house parades highbrow design on a farm-grade budget.

JOHN CONNELL

FROM A DISTANCE, this house is an archetypal cottage with gabled roof, shed-roofed entry, and a chimney. Zoom in and you'll see that the top half of the house is rotated 45 degrees from the bottom, and that walls are covered with corrugated metal roofing while stone siding floats above on the second floor.

Asalvage yard can be a treasure trove for the architect/builder with an open mind and eagle eye. In response to a $50,000 budget, this cottage in Kansas is built almost entirely of materials gathered in salvage-yard harvests. Key hauls included 30-ft.-long steel fink trusses, corrugated steel roofing, green-stone siding, glass blocks, metal windows, metal floor grates, and a manhole cover, complete with the surrounding grating. This mixed bag of materials was transformed into a coherent, clever design with reference to vernacular architecture of both industry and farm.

There's a happy balance of decorum and whimsy . . .

FOUR SALVAGED FINK TRUSSES make a dramatic cover for this Kansas cottage. Custom-sized glass fits between the struts to bring in light during the day and make the house glow at night. More light flows through foursomes of glass block that are punched into plywood box beams forming the second-floor kneewalls.

While it looks simple on paper, the design creates an assortment of niches on both levels and even outside, because the top floor is rotated 45 degrees from the bottom floor. The rotation of the upper floor is reflected in most first-floor walls, including the expansive wall that features a woodstove and two ladder-stairs to the parents' sleeping loft. Ceilings can be low and cozy, as they are over the children's beds and the kitchen, or they can be high, as in the central living space, where

Architect/Builder:
Dan Rockhill
Rockhill and Associates
Location:
Franklin County, Kansas

SALVAGED FINDS INSIDE THE HOUSE include steel and wood ladder-stairs, a yellow maintenance ladder, the metal floor gratings-turned balustrade, and the kitchen cabinets, recently graduated from a high school home-economics classroom.

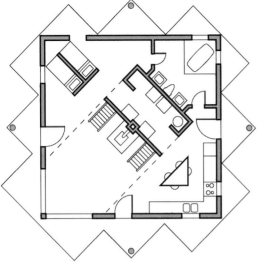

the second floor is cut away to bring in light from the dramatic gable-end glazing. Despite being partially cut away to add space to the living area, the second floor has room for the master bedroom and office space and a children's play loft.

There's a happy balance of decorum and whimsy in this house, inside and out. Exterior elements are symmetrical, colors subdued, and proportions elegant, but the materials are unexpected—for a house, anyway. Metal roofing covers lower walls while stone, the heavier material, floats above, with glass-block portholes punched into the sides. Interior colors are soft and sophisticated, with waves combed into gray stucco wall finish, but spiked with colors from furniture, rugs, and built-ins, such as the bright yellow fire pole. This cottage is concrete evidence that livability and looks are attainable without breaking the bank.

THIS CORNER, OPPOSITE THE KITCHEN, is more sheltered, with kids' bedrooms below and a play loft above. The translucent shoji screen provides varying degrees of privacy without sacrificing light.

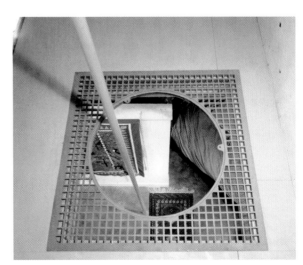

IT'S A QUICK RIDE through the salvaged manhole-cover grating and down the fire pole to the children's bedroom/play area to soothe tempers or ailments.

ONE OF THE ALCOVES created by rotating the second floor is a private loft space for adults, where glass-block windows provide a soft light and diffused view.

A LESSON IN ECONOMY AND GRACE, rotating the top floor 45 degrees provides niches inside and covered entryway space outside. A corrugated-metal shed roof covers the projecting first floor.

A Composition in Balance, Light, and Craft

WHY THIS HOUSE

This house could hardly be simpler in concept, yet I can't imagine a building more carefully refined—both in its intricate detailing and its siting. Bold and calm, reaching beyond itself and yet completely comfortable within its four walls, this home has a power and grace born of basic materials and techniques.

DUO DICKINSON

THIS VIEW FROM THE UNDERSIDE OF THE BOOK LOFT—and just outside the bedroom—focuses on the big stone fireplace, which is shaped like the façade of a house. From here there's just a hint of the kitchen and brightly lit dining bay beyond.

E ven a gently sloping site

can be a challenge when the owners request a house with as few level changes as possible. This hillside in Napa Valley was surrounded by mature hardwoods but was free of trees itself. This gave the architect freedom to use cut and fill to create a flat plane for both house and grounds, making it easy to maneuver both inside and out. The two retaining walls that contain the long, rectangular plateau serve the site, the house, and a separate studio and garage, creating a deliberately composed estate rather than a mere yard with a collection of buildings. The higher wall, especially, has important roles as enclosure for two courtyards, as boundary and heat collector for a lap pool, and as the wall of the house and studio. Inside the house, the stone retaining wall is recessed into the hill to form the shower room.

There's a clear progression from public to private.

Architect:
Eric Haesloop, AIA
Turnbull Griffin Haesloop
Location:
Napa Valley, California

THE BOLD, WHITE-FRAMED WINDOW BAY facing the drive is the first hint that this trim, modest house contains sensational interior spaces. Nothing is haphazard here, from the equally spaced white columns to the neatly aligned vent stacks, a handsome alternative to random holes in the roof.

THIS HIGHER RETAINING WALL forms the edge not only of the courtyard but also the lap pool, the free-standing studio, the back wall of the house, and the side of an entry courtyard and garage. Inside, the wall indents to form the shower.

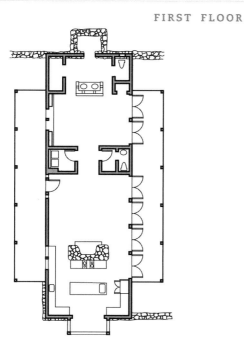

At 1,500 sq. ft., the house is on the small side, and it has a simple rectangular footprint and a single gable roof. But a look inside reveals a series of breathtaking spaces created by making the best use of light, balance, and craftsmanship. Light is balanced by rich color, openness by enclosure, vertical by horizontal, smooth surfaces by repeated structural elements. There's a clear progression from the most public to most private in two directions—from the dining room bay back to the shower notch and from the parking courtyard and front door to the many "back" doors, which open onto the private courtyard. From streetside to hillside, four vertical elements provide focus and surprise: the dining-area bay window, a huge stone fireplace, a dramatic skylight over the book loft, and the skylit shower. Throughout, there's always a connection to the outdoors, where two long porches provide space to sit and enjoy either sunrise or sunset.

THE TALL DINING-AREA BAY WINDOW faces the long driveway, so it is both a beacon for visitors and a lookout for the owners, who can see both an arriving car and the fields below.

THE LIVING SPACE IS SEPARATED from the bedroom by rooms (laundry left, bathroom right) that flank the dramatic skylit hall.

NO DOOR SEPARATES IT FROM THE LIVING SPACE, but the master bedroom feels both protected and important due to the symmetrical layout, sheltering roof, and solid walls. A skylight over the book loft in the foreground provides much light, the skylight over the stone-walled shower adds sparkle, and two sets of French doors at the right lead to the courtyard and lap pool.

THE MASTER BATHROOM IS AROUND THE CORNER from the master bedroom headboard. Its shower is wrapped by the stone retaining wall that bounds the uphill part of the site. A blue mosaic tile floor and generous skylight balance the heaviness of the stone with brilliance and light.

Rambling Farmhouse

A SPRAWLING, FAMILY HOUSE finds its visual precedent in the farmhouse, with green shingle roofs, wide porches, and white clapboard siding.

The prototypical farmhouse

starts out as a tidy box onto which pieces are added over time—a lean-to mudroom, a bedroom addition for a growing family. This northern California house started out rambling, with additions carefully planned but comfortably added, giving it the look of having developed over time. Because it's a single story, ceilings can follow the slope of the gabled roof; this feature, along with nicely proportioned exposed trusses, gives the interior a hint of the flavor of a barn. But painting the exposed structure and board ceiling and providing elegant cabinetry and furnishings keep the interiors light and refined—clearly for people, not horses.

The sprawling layout keeps private and public separate.

In fact, this house has a more formal aspect inside than the exterior would suggest, with symmetrical window placements in the living room and dining

Architect:
Andy Neumann, AIA
Neumann Mendro Andrulaitis
Location:
Sonoma, California

THE MASTER BEDROOM IS A PRIVATE SPACE with its own view and access to the outdoors. A gabled ceiling and exposed structure make reference to rustic barn architecture, but pale paint and furnishings maintain the genteel ambience.

MORE THE LIVING ROOM OF A COUNTRY ESTATE than a farmhouse, this space balances formal symmetry and luxurious furnishings with a few casual wicker pieces.

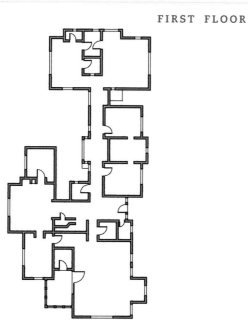

IN CONTRAST WITH THE BRIGHT, light-painted living spaces and bedrooms, this library is cool, dark, and quiet, an ideal place for reading or work.

room, a butler's pantry, and a library with dark, luxurious finishes and furnishings. Hints of casual family life abound, though, with cozy window seats, a comfortable screened porch, and doors leading from bathrooms or bedrooms to the outdoors, making it easy to head to the shower after swimming or playing outdoors.

It's a big house, and the sprawling layout of individual elements keeps private and public areas separate. This allows intimate, comfy spaces and large formal or family spaces to coexist in peace. The bedroom wing can be closed off from the entryway by double doors. Carving up spaces into separate building elements allows for many and varied views across the countryside, including a breath-taking view of a valley, a seasonal creek, and a spectacular ash tree.

FROM A MAGICAL VANTAGE POINT under this ancient ash tree, luxurious spaces and fine French doors take a backseat to a dizzying ride on a rope swing.

THIS HANDSOME TANSU CHEST—
a family heirloom—maintains a
position of honor in an alcove off
the master bedroom suite.

THE KITCHEN/FAMILY SPACE is bright and big, with a
river-rock fireplace, a seating arrangement meant for
conversation, and an ample window seat for reading or
taking in a view of the valley. A second sink in the island
comes in handy for both cooking and gardening tasks.

An Island Retreat
Open to the Future

WHY THIS HOUSE

Working with a restrained palette, Prentiss proves that what makes good design sense for those in a wheelchair can create a compelling environment for the rest of us as well.

JOHN CONNELL

LIGHT AND WARMTH DISTINGUISH the living-room portion of the great room. The concrete floor was cast with a radiant-heat system, and the birch plywood ceiling infuses the room with a golden light. Windows wrap corners and stretch up each side of the fire-place to bring in as much daylight as possible and lighten the mass of the gable end.

For most of us, it's hard to imagine getting older, much less losing the ability to move freely. As a result, little thought is given to designing a house that's accessible. Access for people with limited mobility is mandatory in a public building, but it's attainable in a house, too. The bonus is that a house can be designed to be flexible— so that while it may not have grab bars and ramps at the start, it has wide enough doors, halls, and rooms to fit a future wheelchair.

Alcoves enliven the large room.

Future needs for accessible living drove the design of this house on Orcas Island in Puget Sound. Originally built as a weekend retreat for a woman who had recently been diagnosed with multiple sclerosis, it has become a year-round house because the owner finds it good for her health and peace of mind. She had no physical impairments at the time the house was designed but planned for accommodating a wheelchair in the future. There are no railings or other accoutrements that might be seen in a

Architect:
Geoffrey Prentiss, AIA
Prentiss Architects, Inc.
Location:
Orcas Island, Washington

SITING THE HOUSE ON A SLOPE allows for easy access on grade and opportunity for a far-reaching view on the downhill side, seen here. Simple materials, including yellow-painted fiber-cement panels, concrete block, and off-the-shelf asphalt shingles, are elevated to a high style by an elegant, symmetrical, and well-proportioned façade.

THE BATHROOM HAS AMPLE ROOM for a wheelchair, and the cabinets cantilever to make it easier to get close to the basin. This view is from inside the closet, which has a curtain instead of a door.

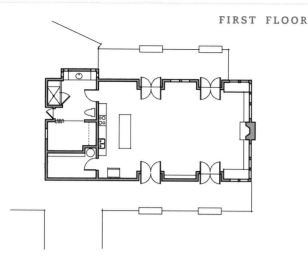

RATHER THAN CARVING UP SPACE to make a separate bedroom, the owner, who had first thought to buy a sleigh bed, now prefers this window seat. Sleeping here is almost like being outdoors under the stars. Blankets are tucked in the open shelves below so the bed can become a window seat during the day.

THE FRENCH DOORS ARE RECESSED to make sheltered entryways and to create alcoves inside. Bookshelves fit into this living-room alcove, giving the room depth and texture.

house used by someone with limited mobility, but doors are wide enough to handle the turning dimension of a wheelchair, aisles are avoided, and, of course, the house is on one level.

It's a simple house—a large room under a single gable serves as kitchen, dining room, workspace, and living room. A spacious bathroom and closet take up the uphill side, opposite the view. But the large room is not itself simple. The French doors are recessed, resulting in alcoves that not only enliven the large room but provide satisfyingly cozy spaces. Bookshelves, window seats, and a sideboard fit into the various alcoves. The outdoors plays a lead role, with large windows, glazed doors, and cantilevered decks on two sides. Decks are finished with cable railings that don't obstruct the view to the Sound, which was, after all, the reason for living here.

BEAUTIFULLY DESIGNED DETAILS add warmth and grace to the modern-style fireplace and window seat. Supported along its length by indigenous madrona branches, the window seat is open to allow easy access. Precast concrete panels, lighter in color than the floor, make an elegant fireplace surround.

SISAL AREA RUGS LIVEN UP the concrete floor and can be easily removed if necessary. Kitchen counters are 4 in. lower than normal, anticipating a time when the owner may need a wheelchair, and wall storage is on open shelving for ease of access.

Fortified against Wind
but Open to View

WHY THIS HOUSE

This tiny home makes a big impact by putting everything on display. Steel, wood, and concrete interweave to make a few basic shapes, which in turn create an elegantly formed home perfectly adapted to its site.

DUO DICKINSON

SHIELDED ON THE SOUTHWEST AND OPEN TO THE NORTHEAST VIEW, the master bedroom faces the newly risen sun and a view of sagebrush and prairie grass. A semiprivate deck, accessible from the bedroom door, is screened from the living-room terrace by a block wall with a simple opening. The oiled steel beam supports 4x6 Douglas fir rafters, which are protected with aluminum-zinc caps.

The inside of a house is usually

where the fragile finishes are—painted drywall or plaster, strip wood flooring, and carpeting. Masonry, concrete, metal, and protected or weather-resistant wood are confined to the exterior. Here's a house that turns that concept on its head. Inside are concrete, concrete block, riveted wood planking—the same finishes that protect the outside—and the same exposed steel and wood structure that's visible outside. Whether it's to welcome in the outdoors or to underpin the sense that the house can weather any storm, this turnabout makes a powerful impression. What softens the look is the contrast between the windward and leeward sides of the house, one being secured and the other unguarded.

The house has a brawny appearance on the windward side.

The house, on an apple orchard at the foothills of the Cascade Mountains and overlooking the Naches Valley in

Architect:
**Craig Curtis, AIA, and
Sian Roberts, AIA
The Miller/Hull Partnership**
Location:
Central Washington

MATERIALS THAT MAKE UP THE EXTERIOR—concrete block, a concrete slab, metal tubing, and heavy Douglas fir planking—find their way inside the house, too. What could be considered tough-as-nails materials are made handsome and even homey by crafting them carefully and giving them high-style detailing and finishes.

A ROLLING ENTRY GATE THAT HELPS SHIELD THE HOUSE from west winds opens to offer a glimpse of the glorious valley view beyond.

On the other side of the entry gate and office, materials lighten up. Because this northeast exposure is calm and secure, the solid walls give way to floor-to-ceiling glass walls. To carry the loads, rafters bear on oiled steel beams supported by steel pipe columns, splayed to imitate orchard props that hold fruit-laden branches.

The stained concrete floor looks the same in the living room as on the terrace, but indoor slabs are warmed by radiant heat. Soft, natural colors of materials and stains mimic native plants: sagebrush, lichen, poplar leaves in autumn, and native grasses.

On the windward side, the bathroom wall is concrete block, but its one small window brings in lots of light. Warm wood cabinets balance the cool tones of the marble countertop and concrete block.

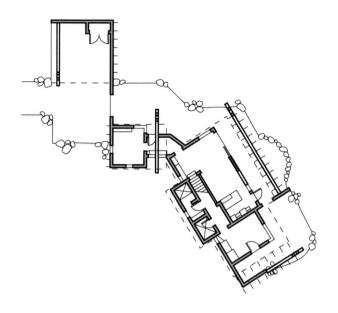

Washington, is exposed to strong winds year-round, not to mention abundant snow and bone-dry heat. Accordingly, it has a brawny appearance on the windward side, which is tucked into the hillside and finished with concrete-block walls, chunky wood planks, a few windows, and even a burly wood gate that rolls closed to keep out the wind and intruders. A single, towering Ponderosa pine beside the house acts as both signpost and shelter. The view of distant hills and the Naches Valley to the northeast is far, wide, and heart-stopping as it overlooks sagebrush and prairie grasses. To take in this view, solid concrete-block walls give way to exposed steel pipe columns and beams and entire walls of windows.

THE KITCHEN IS OPEN TO THE LIVING ROOM and takes on the same palette of landscape colors. Cabinets are Douglas fir, but next to the range the cabinet doors are covered with acid-washed steel panels and embellished with snakelike metal pulls. The bull's-eye was painted on the hood.

New House, Venerable Design

A LONG WOOD MANTEL spans a big fireplace and its flanking bookcases, giving the living room an unmistakable focus. A thickened wall and lowered ceiling between the dining room and living area distinguish the spaces from each other yet maintain openness.

Craftsman-style details

and materials clearly inspired the design of this house, so much so that people often pull into the driveway to ask the owners when it was built, assuming that it's been there for many decades. The ⅔-acre lot is average in size for a Seattle suburb, but it looks wooded because a large grove of alder, maple, and ash was left as intact as possible. Detaching the garage and designing it to look like a carriage house made it easier to maintain tree cover and helps give the house its historic character.

Detaching the garage helps give the house its historic character.

From windows to trim, the house is filled with Craftsman-style touches. Divided lights in windows follow a traditional two-small-over-two-long pattern; door lights are divided into equal-sized rectangles. A substantial fireplace is surrounded with green-gray tile,

Architect/designer:
Johan and Robin Luchsinger, AIA
Baylis Brand Wagner Architects
Location:
Seattle, Washington

RIVER-ROCK COLUMNS, divided-light windows, thick fiberglass shingles, and cedar-shake siding give this new suburban house the look of a Craftsman-style lodge.

A FIRST-FLOOR BEDROOM acts as a guest suite, with vestibule, bathroom, and outside door. The ceiling is vaulted to add light, space, and interest, and wood is featured in details and structure.

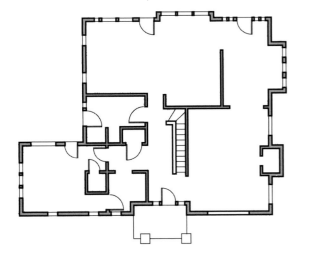

AN ABUNDANCE OF WOOD provides the warm atmosphere in the kitchen/dining area, with cabinets, floors, and trim receiving a natural, low-luster transparent finish. It would have been easier to drywall the short wall perpendicular to the large window over the breakfast table; instead, a slender window boosts both the view and the light.

topped with a broad wood mantel, and flanked by bookcases. Naturally stained wood is featured prominently and beautifully, from the Craftsman-style balustrade to cabinetry, floors, and trim. The owners—also the architect and interior designer—added sweat equity to the building of their house by laying the Craftsman-style stone columns at the entryway, which they set with bits of colored glass found earlier on the property.

Spaces are tied together visually and spatially to make the house look bigger and be more family friendly, but privacy was well considered, too. The two main bedrooms are on the second floor, but a third bedroom, just to the left of the entryway, has its own bathroom and its own exit—perfect for visiting grandparents or an older teenager. Spaces are comfortable and cozy, as in any historic Craftsman-style house, but windows are more abundant, a boon in this often-overcast climate. The entryway is particularly bright and inviting with fixed sidelights and transom windows.

Floor-to-ceiling sidelights and a divided-light transom allow plenty of light into the entryway, and a glazed door beyond offers an enticing view of the backyard trees. Wood floors predominate, but tile at the entry makes a tough, easily cleaned surface for a family that spends time outdoors. A Craftsman-style oak balustrade is one of many period details.

Landscaping work continues on the house, with river rocks destined for edging planting beds and a custom trellis under the guest-room windows that will someday support climbing vines.

A Palette of Design Elements Shapes a Lively House

Under the vast Colorado sky, this cluster of buildings frames and contains the panoramic views, creating powerful backdrops for the human-scaled gardens. The whole is unified by the use of local materials, gabled roofs, and vernacular proportions.

JOHN CONNELL

A VARIED BUT RELATED HANDFUL OF MATERIALS, colors, and shapes mixes to make a house that's both unified and surprising. The white-framed gable end facing the pond contains the dining room, with the living room to the right. At the far right is the gray master bedroom wing with studio above. The guest wing, with its ridge beam sloping upward, is at left.

This Colorado home is a study

in transformation. First, there's the transformation of a flat site with little vegetation into a diverse complex with a pond, abundant landscaping, and a fascinating house at the hub. The site near Aspen has scenic mountain views all around but itself was flat and practically barren of trees, perfect for an extreme makeover. Now there are lush gardens of different character and a pond that sustains a healthy population of fish, birds, and four-footed wildlife. The house pinwheels around and even embraces the various gardens, and throughout there are shifting views of the mountains.

Each chunk of the house sports a different skin.

The building itself is a transformation of a set of materials, colors, and shapes into a multiwinged dwelling, each section a variation on the theme.

Architect:
Scott Lindenau, AIA
Location:
near Aspen, Colorado

THE BREEZEWAY BETWEEN HOUSE AND GARAGE is a room, passageway, and greenhouse in one—and it overlooks the secret garden at right. Exposed building elements make a pleasing rhythm along the wall and roof, from rafters and purlins to window frames to concrete columns outside, formed with sections of galvanized storm pipes.

INSIDE SURFACES ARE SMOOTH, shiny, and more uptown, with polished concrete floors and countertop, streamlined stainless-steel cabinets, and contemporary lighting. Fireplace masonry adds a rustic touch refined by streamlined openings and mantel.

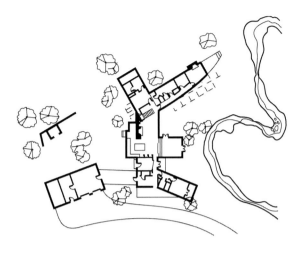

Elements from ranch and farm architecture guided the choices, including the simple gable roof, metal roofing, board-and-batten siding, and the colors, primarily gray, gold, and rust. It's impossible to take it all in at once, which makes the house a constant delight for owner and guests alike. Although each chunk of the house sports a different skin, the overall effect is coherent because the palette sticks to certain rules. For example, all gable ends have symmetrically placed windows and doors, all siding is board-and-batten whether gray or gold, and rust-colored paint on window frames and trim matches the rusty metal roofs.

A VIEW FROM UPSTAIRS takes in the secret garden, the breezeway between garage and house, and the mountains beyond. Even the various landscape walkways match the palette of colors that make up the skin of the house.

What finally ties together the sprawling house is the repetition of two patterns—stripes and grids. Roofing, siding, and columns contribute stripes, and grids are expressed in the exposed roof structure in the breezeway and overhangs and the white-framed window wall that faces the pond. The repetition of proportion, color, pattern, and scale gives this house of many parts a unifying sense of both playfulness and elegance.

IT'S NOT THE CAMERA PLAYING TRICKS—
the roof really does slope up, making a
broad, sheltering overhang to welcome
guests. The roof is fiberglass to allow
plenty of light into the guest room.

THIS DINING ROOM is not just
for meals but for tending
indoor and outdoor plants and
for sheer relaxation.

THIS COZY SPACE is tucked
between the living-room
fireplace masonry and a window wall that overlooks the
secret garden.

A Delicate Balance

The limitations of a tough site make the success of this design all the more spectacular. Light, view, and circulation are choreographed into a seamless weave of hard-edged design in an urban garden.

JOHN CONNELL

HOUSES ALONG THE CANAL are packed like sardines and in view of public walkways on each side of the canal, so privacy is important. On the canal side, windows are large to take in the view, but upstairs bedroom windows can be completely shaded. Landscaping helps buffer the view.

The canals of Venice, California,

may not be as aged and mysterious as those in their namesake city, but they are as magical to live along—not to mention measurably cleaner. Minutes from the Pacific Ocean surf yet sandwiched between an easily navigable waterway and a service road, these canal-side houses are at once intensely urban and close to nature. At 30 ft. by 90 ft., canal lots require that houses fit cheek by jowl. Public walkways border the canals, so maintaining privacy is a high priority. This contemporary house strikes a comfortable balance between public and private by the subtle contrast of space, transparency, light, and color.

Because it's private, the entryway is transparent.

THE NEIGHBORING HOUSE is a mere 6 ft. away, so space is precious. This entryway is at the midpoint of the house facing a blank stucco wall, and it is recessed to make a garden space. It's a semi-private space, so it's glazed to allow in light. The spiral stair offers a direct path to the second-floor suite.

On a narrow site, it's tempting to enter a house through the garage, but this house features the more picturesque solution of directing people along a path to a small, private entry garden, midway through the lot.

Architect:
Glen Irani, AIA
Glen Irani Architects
Location:
Venice, California

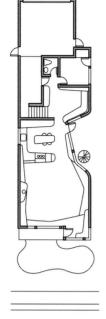

A RAISED THRESHOLD-CUM-DECK is built from fir boards positioned vertically and spaced apart to allow for drainage. The custom-made glass door slides completely open so that inside and outside are one.

The garden itself becomes a gathering place, softly lit by reflected sun that bounces off the neighbor's stucco wall. Because it's a private space, the entryway is transparent, allowing that soft light to brighten the interior as well. At the more public juncture between canal walkway and the living room, a raised threshold-cum-deck creates a boundary between private and public. This deck laps inside and outside, making a conversation platform inside and a subtle barrier outside, even when the tremendous glass door is slid fully open.

Balance between contrasting elements is evident throughout the house. Hard materials such as concrete and flush wood panels are also silky-smooth to touch. Countertops and furniture have curved, people-friendly edges to balance rectilinear windows and panels. Dark concrete and furniture pair with warm, highly figured wood veneer in contrast to white walls, ceilings, and paper light fixtures. The result is a house that's both cozy and dazzling—a joy to come home to, whether by car or canoe.

Different species of wood display subtle differences in color and figure to make a sophisticated fireplace wall in the living room. When the glass door is closed, the raised threshold/deck becomes a bench.

The staircase emulates a tree, with bare treads spiraling around the solid wall like branches around a trunk. Tiny windows punched into the exterior wall provide the luminous glow in the stairwell; the light changes throughout the day.

The threshold/deck runs the full width of the door opening at the edge of the living space to call out the transition between the private house and the garden and public walkway and canal beyond.

All About the Roof

Barnlike in appearance and deceptively simple in plan, this house borrows from the local vernacular but provides a thoroughly contemporary living situation. The variety of the interior spaces is completely consistent with the exterior shapes.

JEREMIAH ECK

BOTH NEARBY HILLS AND THE DISTANT SNOW-CAPPED CASCADE MOUNTAINS provide a model for the roof of this Methow Valley cabin. At present, the house looks like an isolated cabin in the wilderness, but it is part of a planned development and is close to a road for easy access in winter.

The first house on a site,

whether in a suburb or in the wilderness, sets the precedent

for future houses, but from where is its inspiration drawn?

Certainly the landscape makes a compelling muse, especially one

as dramatic as this valley in the eastern foothills of the Cascade

Mountains. The first of a planned develop-

ment, this cabin takes its elemental peaked

form—a steeply gabled roof with shed roofs

appended all around—from the hills and

snow-capped mountains at its doorstep.

Its metal roof, stovepipe chimney, rustic

board-and-batten siding, and broad porches come straight from

the vernacular of the Western homestead.

Wood is abundant, but it's far from rustic.

A steep metal roof with broad overhangs is ideal because

its shape and finish are a response to wind, snow, and sun—no

less prevalent today than a century ago. This house is positioned

to catch the strong breezes, shield the sun, and handle a heavy

load of snow. The interior space is a simple rectangle with a

steep gabled roof, but it's hard to imagine the house without

Architect:
Thomas Lawrence,
Lawrence Architecture
Location:
Methow Valley, Washington

A PORCH ADDS MUCH MORE TO A HOUSE than its cost would imply. This porch wraps around the entire house to allow for views on all sides, making room for bikes in summer and skis in the winter. Aesthetically, the porch is the element that gives the house its cheerful character and appealing proportions. Cedar board-and-batten siding and a metal roof give the house a rustic look.

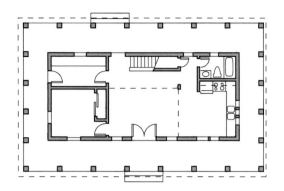

the encircling porches and continuous shed roof, which transform the basic box into an appealing, even endearing form that's a welcome sight after a hectic week in the city.

Inside the house, the homestead vernacular is tempered by a modern aesthetic where wood is abundant, but it's far from rustic. Wood floors, trim, and furniture are smooth and streamlined, and no country-cottage knick-knacks clutter the look. The second floor is carved away over the living room to provide more vertical space and to maintain a connection between the living space and the office/guestroom space upstairs. If owners and guests aren't already outside on one of the four porches, they can take in views to the horizon on all four exterior walls. Happily, the house sits on a three-acre site at the edge of a forest that is forever protected, so this cabin will always be a pioneer even when the neighborhood gets crowded.

WHETHER FROM ONE OF THE PORCHES or from inside the cabin, the views are awe-inspiring. Building the house on a flat site allows for easier access in the winter, not only to the road but to a cross-country ski trail just 100 yards away.

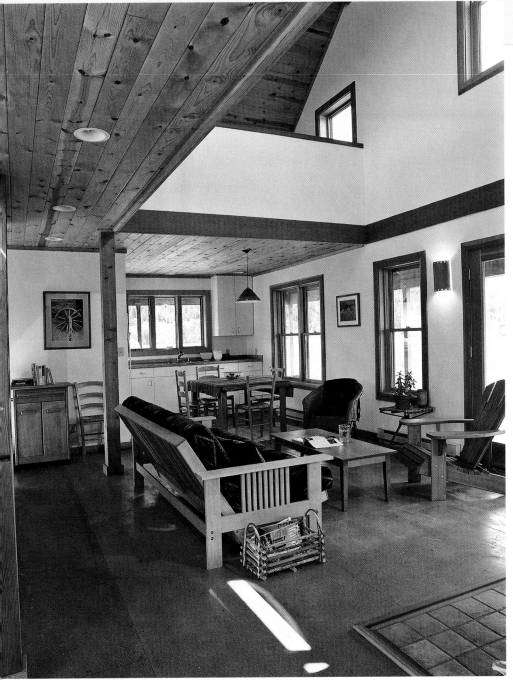

For economy and simple good looks, off-the shelf materials make a good choice. Floors are either brick or clear-finished processed wood panels, kitchen cabinets are off-the-shelf plastic laminate, doors are fir, and windows are standard-sized energy-efficient aluminum clad.

A portion of the living space is open to the second floor to make the space more generous but also to allow for a bit of privacy without seclusion. Upstairs office and bedroom spaces cover circulation space and the kitchen/dining area below to add a sense of intimacy.

A Big House Thinks Small

THE HEART OF THE ACTION in this big Oregon house, the kitchen has both cozy and wide-open spaces. A side door opens at left on axis with the path to the stair and hall at right; this divides the kitchen into working space for food preparation and quiet space for desk work at left or eating in the cozy nook at right. A door and window keep the dining room in close contact.

It takes a little forethought

to make a big house a comfortable scale for everyday living. All too often, big houses are filled with big rooms that are great for parties but overpowering for quiet times. One way to allow for gatherings but still make room for a family—or just one person—to feel at home is to shave slices off rooms or add nodes onto rooms to make alcoves. This 3,600-sq.-ft. house in Oregon is layered with alcoves of all kinds, with covered porches and private balconies, sleeping nooks, eating niches, corners to read in, and bays for conversation.

No space is a simple rectangular volume.

The basic shape of the house is a simple rectangle with an asymmetrical gabled roof, but a series of shed-roofed dormers pop up to make bedrooms and a common room. Inside, this configuration makes niches under the gabled roof and higher ceilings under the dormer, which add up to a rich variety of spaces. Two spaces are carved out of the roof to form balconies, one private and one off the

Architect:
James W. Givens Design
Location:
Eugene, Oregon

A VIEW OF THE LIVING-ROOM commons corner of the house shows its basic gable-roofed shape. A series of gabled dormers project from the gable to house the common room and bedrooms.

FAMILY MEMBERS AND GUESTS ALIKE love this alcove, perfect for a restful afternoon reading the newspaper and taking in a lovely view of the hills. From here there's a view of the fireplace and living-room conversation area, but it's easy enough to close the curtain and enjoy some peace.

THE BACK-DOOR ENTRYWAY is a sunny spot, comfortable enough for settling in with newspaper and coffee. The house is built on a hill, so to allow on-grade entry, this bay is placed just off a landing in the staircase. It makes a welcome side trip.

THE ENTRANCE TO THE LIVING ROOM comes immediately into the fireplace inglenook on the north wall, while the more communal portion of the room is opposite the fireplace at the bright bay window. A bed alcove at left offers an optional view of the fireplace.

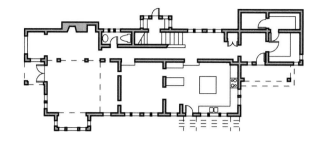

common room; these add visual depth, too. The complexity established by the alternating pattern of dormer on background gable is tempered by common materials and colors. The upper level is finished with clear-stained wood shingles, while the bottom level is covered with a smoother finish, natural-stained clapboards.

No space inside is a simple rectangular volume. Along one wall of the kitchen, a desk nook and an eating niche add a layer of intimacy, called out by a lower ceiling. The living room has a series of spaces that break down the scale of a large room, from the inglenook entrance to a brightly lit bay at the opposite end, with a cozy sleeping/resting alcove just off one corner. From here, a family member or guest has a view of the fire and a view of the hills, and the option to close off the room with a curtain.

THE WALL BETWEEN THE DINING ROOM and living room is made thick with bookshelves and detailed framework around a leaded-glass window. This quiet alcove is set off by a trimmed opening supported by columns.

THIS SECOND-FLOOR ALCOVE offers space for a sleepover friend or cousin, or just quiet room for reading or playing. It's tucked under the main gable roof, while the rest of the room is expanded by a shed dormer.

Rural Shapes, Uptown Details

THE AMERICAN GRAIN ELEVATOR and Japanese farmhouse elements were the inspiration for this rural house, designed for a three-acre site in northern California. The house looks modest in size, but inside, spaces are generous and varied enough for a family of six.

A mix of well-crafted materials and contrasting colors.

Built in the rolling hills north

of San Francisco, this house inherited its looks from rural prototypes, with a roofline that evokes the Japanese farmhouse and a tower patterned after the American grain elevator. Even the siding—that old farm standby, corrugated metal—gives a rural flavor. But a closer look reveals a detour from the forthright design of most farm buildings. A thick concrete wall cuts through the house on a slant, and the tower roof tilts at a rakish angle.

That concrete wall signals the entryway, itself the beginning of a tapered hallway that slices through the house dividing public from private. The living, dining, and kitchen spaces are delineated not by walls but by a post-and-beam structure, and the spaces are tied together by a high gabled ceiling, making for a space that's at once unrestrained and orderly. An enormous island makes a fourth wall for the open kitchen without obstructing views and conversation. This expansive public space is balanced by several small, cozier spaces

Designer:
Fu-Tung Cheng
Cheng Design
Location:
Northern California

CONCRETE MAKES AN EXCITING APPEARANCE inside and outside the house, with holes cast in the walkway for grasses and the interior wall of the main hallway angling out to call out the entry.

THIS VIEW, FROM THE CONCRETE-WALLED HALLWAY, shows the high-ceilinged great room with living space on the right and dining/kitchen space on the left. Wood, concrete, and steel play off each other throughout: An inlay of wood-strip flooring appears to float between two concrete slabs and steel columns clad in fir.

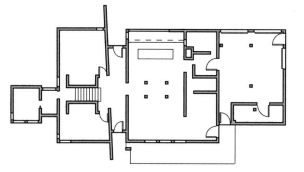

A LARGE, LIGHT-FILLED BATHROOM for the family's four children features a cast-concrete floor and countertop as well as kid-height hooks for towels.

without exposed structure, including a family room under a lowered ceiling and bedrooms tucked into the private wing and served by bathrooms stacked in the tower.

A mix of well-crafted materials and contrasting colors adds charm and surprise—especially to living spaces. Concrete, steel, and wood strike an exhilarating, elegant balance on columns, floors, countertops, and walls. Bedrooms present a more understated image, with conventional drywall walls, carpeted floors, and warm, cozy colors.

THE GREAT ROOM gets both its drama and its serenity from the structure and detailing. The "wow" factor comes from a high, exposed roof structure and carefully detailed metal-and-wood joinery, along with a roomful of views across rolling hills. Coziness comes from the orderly columns and the lighting.

WHILE THE MAIN LIVING SPACES are alive with an exposed structure and a mix of materials, bedrooms are softer and simpler. The master bedroom is tucked under a multilevel gabled roof, and a built-in dresser fits into the knee-wall space.

A MASSIVE CONCRETE-AND-WOOD ISLAND delineates the edge of the kitchen space. The cast-in-place countertop features inlaid objects, such as the fossilized nautilus shell in the foreground.

A Well-Crafted Cottage

WHY THIS HOUSE

Could this house be any simpler? A gridded plan, a basic shape, and a bared structure— it's in the subtle enrichments of craft and detail that this home becomes delightful.

DUO DICKINSON

THIS SMALL HOUSE IN TOWN makes its presence known with a steeply sloped front-facing gable, a bright yellow door, and three yellow squares spaced above the porch roof. The crisp, smooth green and bright yellow surfaces balance the rough gray of cedar wall and roof shingles.

When a modest budget

and a tight site call for a small house with a simple configuration, it doesn't follow that the quality of materials has to be less, too. In fact, money invested in good-quality materials and craftsmanship is better spent in a small house as labor costs are reduced. This cottage in Eugene, Oregon, is proof that fine materials and beautifully crafted spaces add volumes to the livability and joy of any house, regardless of size.

Small details resonate far beyond the cost of materials.

Wood is in great abundance in this house, which is no surprise for a Northwest dwelling. Naturally, Douglas fir plays a big role. Its fine, straight figure and rich color add elegance and warmth throughout the house. Floor joists are Douglas fir, as are ceiling boards; upstairs, knotty pine paneling makes a more informal look for

Architect:
Howard Davis
Location:
Eugene, Oregon

A CLOSE LOOK REVEALS HOW ELEGANT Douglas fir is as a paneling material, with its straight, close figure and rich red-gold color. The oak stair and floor are a complementary golden tone. The window trimmed Craftsman style looks into the studio of the owner/architect.

LIKE THE REST OF THE HOUSE, the dining corner is finished with lots of wood, handsomely detailed and well finished. Painted wood shelves make a unified mass, broken only by a tiny window peeking through.

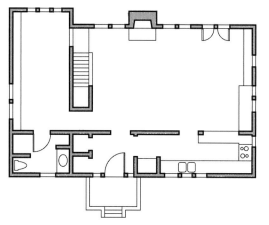

FIRST FLOOR

ceilings. Some of the wood, such as that in the shelves, is painted to make it less obvious, but most is finished to retain its natural look. While it may cost a bit more for higher-grade wood, and it takes extra care to work, naturally finished wood actually ages well, as small dings and discolorations aren't as evident as on painted surfaces.

It's not just the materials that make the grade here. Small details add style and character to the house, even if they aren't immediately evident. One such example is the transom window placed over most operable windows and over doors. The window adds light, style, height, and interest not only to the windows but also to walls both inside and out. Another tiny feature is the pattern of three small yellow squares above the entry and matching yellow squares centered in the tile fireplace. These small details resonate far beyond the cost of materials and labor.

THE VIEW FROM THE SECOND FLOOR looks out over gardens and densely wooded backyards. Tucked partly under the roof, the balcony is framed to give a sense of security and coziness and paneled with the same knotty pine that finishes off the upstairs ceilings.

DOUGLAS FIR FLOOR JOISTS and clear Douglas fir ceiling boards add warmth and texture to the ceilings throughout the first floor. Living-room windows, like most in the house, are topped with divided-light transom windows for an extra fillip of craftsmanship and light.

KEEPING THE STAIR OPEN to the living/dining room makes the space seem larger and turns the stair into a decorative element. The studio view into the living space allows for shared view, light, and curiosity. Green tiles and trim on the fireplace add zing to warm tones of wood and yellow paint; the four yellow tiles recall the yellow squares over the front door.

THE HOUSE IS SMALL, but there's still room for a semipublic space upstairs. This library flanks the open space; the balcony is opposite. A small bedroom at right and bathroom down the hall are the fully private spaces.

Weaving House into Landscape

REPEATED WOOD ELEMENTS and stone walls and chimney bond this bayside house to its rocky, wooded landscape. Deep overhangs and a low profile make a sheltering roof that defers to the towering trees.

Two wings break up the apparent size.

The heft of a timber frame

post-and-beam structure can be a satisfying sight, but an exposed-wood structure of milled lumber can be just as expressive. This house in Washington State is built of standard-sized lumber bundled and layered to imitate the lean seaside tree species in the surrounding forest. Built to replace a dilapidated family cabin on a ledge overlooking Sequim Bay, the 4,500-sq.-ft. house is certainly not cabin-sized, yet the weaving together of a graceful wood structure and massive stone masonry gives it a presence that respects the land. Repetitious elements—bundled posts, doubled beams, ribbons of windows—create a rhythm that evokes tree trunks with patches of sky and water between. Columbia River Gorge basalt forms retaining walls, chimneys, and walkways, and the tightly fit stones create a solid mass that imitates the ledge itself.

Architect:
James Cutler, FAIA
Cutler Anderson Architects
Location:
Sequim Bay, Washington

FROM THE WATERSIDE, the house rises from the ground wrapped with three basalt masonry walls. The outer wall supports a stair, the inner shelters a ramp, and the tall wall is a parapet for the outdoor court.

THE GREAT ROOM AND HALLWAY open to the outdoor living court, the heart of the house, which faces the bay. Windows on the three surrounding walls and 8-ft.-tall glass doors keep the space visible and easy to access from inside. But the court itself isn't visible from the entryway; high, narrow windows—visible in the hallway—allow only a sneak peek.

KITCHEN, DINING, AND LIVING SPACES combine to make a welcoming great room, well defined by cabinetry, window placement, and structure. Wood predominates inside, but variations in color, figure, finish, and fasteners make for a complex composition.

IN CELEBRATION OF MATERIALS AND JOINERY, wood posts are bundled and stacked with stainless-steel fasteners and protective plates. Colors of exterior materials echo the landscape, including the red-gold of cedar lumber, the warm gray of basalt, and the dull green of the window frames.

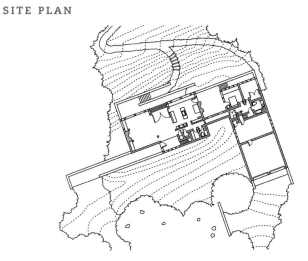

Even the layout of the house defers to the landscape. Two wings break up the apparent size, with a larger, transparent leg that contains a long kitchen, dining, and living space topped by a master bedroom suite, and a more opaque wing that shelters a guest suite, garage, and recreation room. Visitors park just southeast of the entry, then walk up one of two parallel stone-walled stairways to a well-covered entryway. Under the low, sheltering roof is a generous two-story space with glass at both levels. The impact of the bay view—and of the graciousness of the great room—is visible only after moving through the entry hall.

THE FORESTLIKE REPETITION of exposed wood posts appears around the master bathroom, too, but with an infill of clear and translucent glass separating the bath from the two-story entry space and the bedroom.

Completely hidden from the entry side, an outdoor court joins the two wings at the core of the house. The court is sheltered by the wings yet is completely visible to the interior and easy to reach through generous 8-ft. glass doors. A massive basalt chimney—twin to the chimney anchoring the public wing—is the focus of the outdoor court. Whether lit by the glow of a fire or the glow from the warmly lit wood-rich interior, the court at night is as magnetic as any campfire in the woods.

A Craftsman Bungalow Pays Homage to Its Forebears

This house is a modern essay on a classic historical style. Architect Gelotte has not only faithfully replicated the siting, massing, material detailing, and window arrangement of the Craftsman bungalow, he has even maintained the essential features of the layout.

JOHN CONNELL

THE CENTRAL STAIR DEFINES THE EDGE of the living room with its decorative gridded balustrade and built-in, tansulike drawers, which make beautiful use of an often-underused space. A wood-paneled wall at left separates the living room from the entryway yet allows light and view to travel through.

THE HOUSE NESTLES INTO THE HILLSIDE, looking as ageless as the landscape. Northwest redwood clapboards are stained caramel, and shingles are bark brown. The driveway continues to the back of the house, where the garage is sited—a refreshing alternative to the typical suburban house with garage front and center.

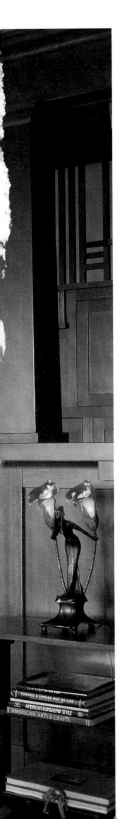

What defines the American

Craftsman-style house is an intense respect for the craft of building, from the making of tiles and trim to the construction of the house itself. Designers of the early 20th-century versions—the Greene brothers of Pasadena, California, are the most notable style makers—were influenced by the philosophy of the English Arts and Crafts movement and the purity of the Japanese wood house.

Craft is celebrated, so joinery is exaggerated.

The Craftsman style has remained immensely popular for many decades, and it is the inspiration for this Seattle bungalow, built on a hillside overlooking Lake Washington.

Like its Craftsman ancestors, this house displays a reverence for natural materials and colors, exposed structural members and joinery, and healthy, free-flowing space. Nestled into the hills, the bungalow maintains a

Architect:
Curtis Gelotte, AIA
Curtis Gelotte Architects
Location:
Seattle, Washington

MUCH HEFTIER THAN THE roof load requires, these bundled square columns symbolize strength, stability, and shelter. Joinery is exposed in a celebration of woodworking craft.

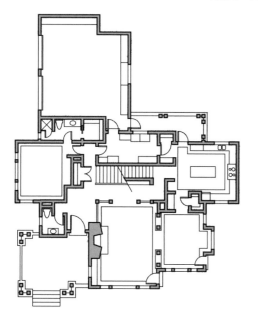

low, unassuming profile, with shallow roofs and deep eaves and colors that blend with the landscape—brown shingles, dark caramel clapboard, and olive-drab trim. Although the house is a full two stories high, upstairs rooms and roofs are configured individually to break up the mass and keep the house humble. Notice, though, that all upstairs rooms have large windows with a view of the lake below.

The process of craft is celebrated here, so joinery is exaggerated. Porch columns are solid, even hefty, and tapered to show how structural loads increase from capital to base. Details and ornamentation are either linear and abstract, such as the stair balustrade, or organic and curved, as in light fixtures and on accent tiles. The happy result of focusing on fine craftsmanship and materials, on natural colors, and on keeping spaces open and flowing is that this Craftsman house is comfortable, intimate, and a constant pleasure to live in.

THIS HANDSOME BALUSTRADE is a copy of a stair in a 1907 San Francisco house, itself an homage to the Arts and Crafts movement that originated in the British Isles.

THE LIVING ROOM, ENTRYWAY, AND DINING ROOM share space and light not only at doorways but also above half-height walls that double as display cabinets. The tray ceiling is paneled in Douglas fir and trimmed with crown molding that conceals recessed lights. This detail was rarely seen in original Craftsman homes but looks completely at home here.

THE DINING ROOM IS A MIX of pale cream, golden light, and dark-stained Douglas fir. Most of the woodwork is finished with a semitransparent stain that contains a bit of pigment, which provides color and richness yet allows the grain of the wood to be seen.

THE FIREPLACE WAS AN IMPORTANT ELEMENT in the Craftsman home. This detail reveals elegant Douglas fir woodwork and finely chiseled, handmade accent tiles, demonstrating the Arts and Crafts philosophy that ornament imitates nature.

Earth, Sky, and Water

Part skeleton, part tent, this house makes sculpture out of structure and transforms the natural world into the built environment with a minimum of steps. The home meshes site, structure, and a way of living with nature.

DUO DICKINSON

THIS SOD-ROOFED ISLAND HOUSE looks as if it were extruded vertically from the ground with the earth from the site still clinging to the roof. Its simple shape and low eaves belie the complexity, scale, and drama inside.

The house is grounded to its ancestral roots.

Once the land of an ancient

indigenous people, this dramatic island site is now home to owners sympathetic with the landscape and history. After living on the Gulf of Georgia island in British Columbia off and on for 20 years, they decided to build a timber frame house imbued both with respect for the sacredness of the site and with awe for the majesty of the view. But rather than tower over the site to get the best views, the house hunkers low with the landscape. In fact, there's not much outside the house to prepare a visitor for the drama inside, where skilled timber and masonry craftsmanship, flowing spaces, and awe-inspiring views come together.

The timber frame is made of salvaged Douglas fir, with columns left round but peeled and finished, and most beams squared off and joined. There's a corridor running the length of the house, but it's more than just a hallway, with curved, laminated

ARCHITECTS AND OWNERS AGREED that the basic shape of the house should refer to a longhouse built near this site by the ancient Saanich people. The traditional shape is rendered in a collage of ancient and modern materials—peeled columns, stone and sod, glue-laminated beams, and tempered glass.

THE TOP-LIT CENTRAL CIRCULATION SPACE links front to back and side to side. This spot is down a few steps from the entryway and on grade with the bedroom wings, but not all the way down into the living area, where the view of the gulf is the most dramatic.

Architect:
Blue Sky Design
Location:
Gulf of Georgia, British Columbia

WOOD SCARF JOINTS connect timbers to make a continuous beam.

THIS MASSIVE FIREPLACE was built from sandstone that was quarried on the island, shipped to the site by barge, and cut and laid by a master mason. The raised hearth skirts the length of the masonry edifice to provide ample informal seating.

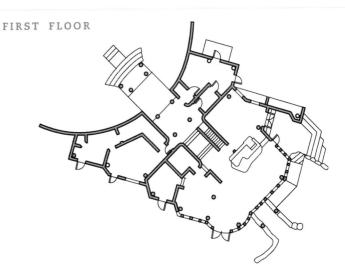

beams that are both structural and decorative. Clear-glass panels allow plenty of light from the often-overcast sky.

The house follows the slope of the site, and it has very few square corners, so each rafter is a different length and pitch. To allow for the best view, columns and major beams are set in from the exterior walls, and roof rafters cantilever from the beams. This allows exterior walls to be nonbearing and free to have as much glass as possible, giving the feeling of being outside and inside at the same time. Private spaces are located on the uphill side and have fewer windows and more privacy, while living spaces are open to the breathtaking, often haunting view. But certain elements, such as a massive fireplace and low eaves, keep the house and its inhabitants grounded to its ancestral roots.

THIS VIEW OF THE CENTRAL PASSAGEWAY shows how the floor level steps down with the slope of the land. The spine is well lit by clear panels fit between laminated curved roof joists. A continuous beam stays level and runs throughout the house, while the floor level steps down.

THE HEAVY ENTRANCE DOOR is hinged a foot from the outside edge to better carry the weight of the door and to add a visual twist to the process of entering. The timber frame itself becomes the door frame. Cleverly designed wood hardware is an example of the fine craftsmanship throughout.

A Childhood Home Reborn

Sometimes the hardest projects end up looking the most effortless. Taking a generic ranch and infusing it with light while at the same time incorporating the gift of its site allows a stock home to fit its occupants.

DUO DICKINSON

THIS IS NOT A REMODEL FOR THE FAINT-HEARTED. A well-built but dark 1960s ranch—still visible in the center—was beefed up, brightened, and transformed into a Craftsman-style house with more space, a formal look, and an eye for a spectacular view of Puget Sound. Craftsman-style details such as gray shingles and gently sloped walls unify new and old.

It's a no-brainer to knock down

a small house on a hot property, but it took insight and courage to transform a dark but well-built 1960s ranch into this stunning house, now an asset to its setting. The owner of the house grew up in it and loved the place itself, but she and her husband preferred a more formal style, more distinct rooms, a better flow of space, and more space, period. Just as important was to better take in the spectacular view of Puget Sound, complete with seasonal sightings of whales and bald eagles.

Beams and paneling were brightened with white paint.

The solution? With their architect, the couple transformed the 2,000-sq.-ft. ranch into a 3,200-sq.-ft. Craftsman Shingle-style both inside and out. Doors and windows were retrimmed in Craftsman style, and the brick and clapboard

Architect:
Bret Drager
Drager Gould Architects
Location:
near Tacoma, Washington

THIS WING ONCE HAD THREE BEDROOMS clustered around one bathroom. A new second-floor master-bedroom suite provides more space and a much better view. Formerly encircled by a simple lawn, the house is now shielded and enhanced streetside by small trees, shrubs, and ground cover.

EVEN THOUGH WALLS WERE REMOVED to improve circulation and add light, rooms have actually become more distinct by framing openings with elegantly designed wide-board trim and by adding a profiled trim at door-head height. Dark-stained wood paneling and beams are now white like all the trim, an elegant look with the darker cream walls.

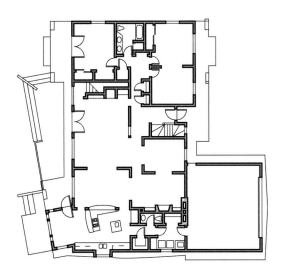

INTERIOR WINDOWS DISPERSE LIGHT into interior spaces such as the former den, now fit with a new gas fireplace to make a cozy space that can be closed off with pocket doors.

siding was replaced with gray shingles. The roof was raised in two sections not only to add a master-bedroom suite but also to expand the kitchen vertically and add much-needed light to the den and kitchen by way of clerestory windows. The additional height gives the house a more formal look and makes it easier to take in the view. The living-room fireplace, smack in the middle of the south wall facing the water, was replaced with French doors. A kitchen-side covered porch was enclosed and given a 5-degree tilt to give the breakfast room an unobstructed view.

But the ranch remains, making remodeling a much thriftier choice than building from scratch. Most of the original structure was retained. Doorways were often enlarged or filled in to redirect traffic and to better distinguish private from public space, making the house both more comfortable and more expansive. Wood-paneled sloped ceilings were left in homage to the ranch style, but beams and paneling were brightened with white paint. A vital part of the ranch was kept alive when the builder saved the jamb where the owner's parents had recorded her height and remounted it in the basement playroom next to a corresponding jamb. That's where the couple charts their own growing daughter.

AN EATING NOOK takes over space that was once a covered porch and deck. A higher ceiling makes a bright, delightful space, and the nook is angled to a clear view of Vashon Island. This is where the family spends most of its daylight hours when not outside on the new, expansive decks.

Summer Camp, All Year Long

SIMPLE GABLED RECTANGLES flanking a pool make up a casual family house in Napa Valley. A two-level cross gable allows for a larger living space and creates a shaded alcove alongside. The single-level portion is rammed earth, while the two-storied section, along with the sleeping building at left, are stick built and finished with barn siding. Galvanized metal roofing adds to the rural image.

Ten acres in Napa Valley

would be the perfect site for a vintner's villa, Tuscan-style, with a courtyard and fountains. Or would it? Maybe a local architectural precedent would be more fitting, such as a century-old California barn with a simple gabled metal roof and rough vertical siding. This family home draws inspiration from both house types to make a casual home for year-round living, indoors and out. The archetypal barn lends its simple, practical gabled shape and tough, locally available materials, such as galvanized metal roofing and vertical cedar siding. The sheltering L-shaped plan with separate buildings joined by a breezeway stems from the Mediterranean country house, where the sun is screened but the weather is too glorious to stay indoors.

The outdoors is the real living space.

The goal of retaining all the trees set the stage for locating the two building parts just south of a grove of gnarly oaks, with the two most venerable oaks framing

Architect:
Cass Calder Smith Architecture
Location:
Napa Valley, California

THIS BREEZEWAY, at the end of a walkway from remote parking, is the threshold of both house and grounds. It joins the living building, left, and sleeping building and allows for shaded dining or relaxing.

FRENCH DOORS OPEN the master bedroom to the pool. A vine-covered trellis and a moss-and-stone carpet make this a peaceful space. To the right is the breezeway and a view of the giant oaks that frame the entry.

THERE ARE MANY WAYS TO GET DIRTY or end up with aching muscles, so an outdoor bath/shower is a blessing. It's well situated beside the tranquil oak grove and a door away from the laundry and bathroom areas that serve the two bedrooms and sleeping loft.

ROOF HEIGHTS INDICATE DIFFERENT FUNCTIONS. At left is the midheight sleeping wing, which has a small loft space for spillover sleeping. A low roof covers the breezeway, kitchen/dining area, and bathroom node at far right. The living space with workspace loft above has the tallest profile, as it's the domain of both community and privacy.

RAMMED-EARTH WALLS are not only a naturally warm color but are also cool in summer and warm in winter. The radiant-heat concrete floor adds to cool-weather comfort. A steel ridge beam, steel collar tie, and steel door lintel allow for more space and a wider door opening. The simple addition of crossed muntins gives ordinary sliding glass doors more distinction.

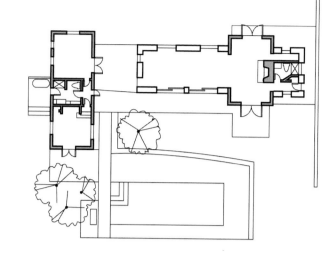

the breezeway, which doubles as outdoor seating. Easy upkeep, informal living, and a quick route to the outdoors determined the low, gabled rectangles and the joining of kitchen, dining, and living spaces into one room that faces the pool and hillside. A cross gable allows the living space to expand and creates more outdoor alcoves. The living building has rammed-earth walls, which are lovely in color and low in maintenance, not to mention cool in summer and warm in winter. The sleeping building is stick-built but with not a sheet of drywall anywhere; cedar paneling covers walls, and ceilings are simply exposed sheathing or loft-floor decking.

For easy access, the house is kept to one story, save for two lofts for overflow sleeping or private workspace. Informality drives design, with no formal entry, a shared bathroom between bedrooms, an outdoor shower, and canvas curtains serving as closet doors and room divider. Instead of a dining room, there's enough space in the great room for a table and a collection of oak chairs, each slightly different. But a look out of any window tells why the focus isn't on elaborate indoor space. The outdoors is the real living space, whether in the many shaded alcoves, the surrounding grounds, or the fields beyond.

KITCHEN, DINING, AND LIVING SPACES share a room, but walls and ceiling heights define the various parts. A cross-gabled rectangle enlarges the living room and helps shelter the outdoor porch. A working/sleeping loft above the living room makes the space more intimate.

Tiny Cottages with a Generous Outlook

WHY THIS HOUSE

Designing a small house is difficult; designing a community of small houses is even more so. Like a boat, every element must not only be useful but also, as here, beautiful.

JEREMIAH ECK

COTTAGES, GREEN GARDENS, AND FENCES are diminutive, but each is in scale with the other to make a cohesive and charming community on an island in Washington state. Though the houses share similar roof shapes, materials, and trim details, they're by no means cookie-cutter likenesses.

It's easy to design a big house

with spacious rooms and grand details. A tougher task is to make a small house appear roomy, well proportioned, and inviting. This community of eight cottages on less than an acre on Whidbey Island, Washington, has met that task with minimum space but maximum attention to detail and layout.

The cottages are each roughly 600 sq. ft. to 650 sq. ft., plus a loft and a porch. Side by side, they bound a green and a garden, and parking fits in two small lots along one side behind the houses, along with storage lockers and a workshop. Owners and guests park, then walk into the central common and garden before heading to the individual cottages. Although the cottages are small, front porches are generous so that occupants can spend time enjoying the outdoors

Space is precious but not skimpy.

Architect:
Ross Chapin, AIA
Ross Chapin Architects
Location:
Whidbey Island, Washington

TO MAKE A SMALL BEDROOM CHARMING and more spacious vertically, floor joists and loft decking are left exposed. The window above the alcove seat, placed high for privacy, provides a wonderfully diffused light that's amplified by the white-painted beadboard.

LIGHT FROM THE EATING SPACE infuses this small kitchen, while small design touches add spice and cheer. Drawer pulls are shaped like vegetables, and the red-and-beige linoleum floor is matched by the single-row checkered backsplash.

THE BEST SPOT IN EACH COTTAGE is the alcove with built-in benches and table. It's a light-infused, intimate space for dining, working, or talking. While the space is small, windows on three sides increase the perceived size immeasurably.

IT WOULD HAVE BEEN EASY TO SPEC off-the-shelf cabinetry for these small cottages, but it's much more effective to offer custom details, such as the paneling on doors, the hefty bin pulls, and painted beadboard.

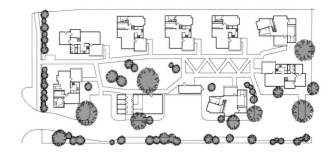

or conversing with neighbors. Cottages are unified by Arts and Crafts detailing and proportions such as front-facing gables with shallow-sloped roofs, earth-toned siding, and chunky woodwork built up from stock lumber sizes.

Space is precious here, but not skimpy. To make the most of a small footprint, walls are bumped out or recessed while alcoves stretch the view and provide coziness or storage. In each cottage, a bay window offers seating and amplifies daylight, recessed shelves under a stair make an elegant mini-library, and a loft is tucked over the bedroom. The loft adjoins the living space, not only to add space but also to lengthen the view and bring light into the living room from above. Trim is used in abundance for framed openings, stairs, cabinetry, and exteriors to a degree rarely seen in such tiny houses, adding to the appeal of the cottages. In the spirit of community, sustainable and environmentally friendly materials prevail, including formaldehyde-free particleboard floors, fiber-cement board siding, and reclaimed Sitka spruce for interior paneling.

LOFT SPACE ADDS 200 SQ. FT. to the total (that's a 33 percent boost in floor area), making room for a home office or retreat. Access to the loft is via a ship's ladder, which conserves space and seems right for an island house.

We invited three of the architects who helped select the **50 houses** to write a short essay on a residential design topic close to their hearts. Fortuitously, this also gives us the opportunity to showcase some of the houses that **John Connell, Duo Dickinson**, and **Jeremiah Eck** have designed in recent years.

This section concludes with an essay by **Richard Hayes**, Managing Director of **Knowledge Resources for the AIA** in Washington, DC, on the value of using an architect, followed by a listing of all the architects featured in the book.

THE
Architects

JOHN CONNELL

DUO DICKINSON

JEREMIAH ECK

People Make the Place

The best home designs can only be understood through the people who inspire them and the lives they live within them. What distinguishes the houses collected in this book is more than just the shapes and materials used in their construction. It's the personalities so clearly legible in the designs. From the siting to the massing, from the choice of materials to the level of detailing, and from the craftsmanship to the landscaping, each of these houses reveals a signature collaboration among people sharing a common architectural vision.

Houses are perhaps our most fundamental expression of self, the stage on which our unique story is cast. The choices we make in our houses are what give them personality, character, and drama. The idea of a "normal" or standard house is as ridiculous as the notion of a standard personality. Thus, cookie cutter "units" and oversized trophy homes can never compete with houses specifically tailored to personal preferences and lifestyle. Without exception, interesting people make interesting houses; they simply can't help it. And occasionally, when the varied personalities of homeowner, architect, and builder find a synergistic stride, the house becomes more than

THIS EXPERIMENTAL BUILDING looked afresh at every aspect of home design, but without a homeowner to inspire the vision, it would remain more sculpture than residence.

TO SHAPE THE DESIGN OF AN "OLD" FARMHOUSE, the client and architect first scripted an imaginary building history, spanning several generations. The resulting house expresses qualities of the homeowners that were woven into that saga.

THE PASSAGE OF TIME
is expressed by the geo-
logical strata suggested
in the fireplace design,
reinforcing the timeless
quality of family gathered
around the hearth.

HOMEOWNERS WITH CONTEMPORARY LIFESTYLES
often want to be housed in traditional designs.
Undoubtedly, this helps them connect with an era
when the house was a more detailed portrait of the
family's life.

expressive—it becomes architecture, maybe even art.

Residential architecture will always be much more than just striking patterns of color, material, and shape. At its best, it becomes a three-dimensional language that can express the personal values and dreams of those who embrace it. It's fundamental to the human experience. Seen in this light, the houses collected here are a testament to those who would make a better world, live a better life, and revel in the timeless practice of "making a place."

Breaking the Rules

WINDOWS AND ENTRIES don't always have to follow a predictable pattern. Windows should correspond to what's going on inside (guess where the stair is in the top photo), and entries need to respond to the site.

Predictability seldom makes for the best results in architecture. Beyond inducing boredom, design by rote often compromises usefulness and efficiency. For example, if you build your house directly at the end of a driveway, there's no way to see the site for the garage. And if the public side of a home always faces the street, the site's views, slope, trees, and other natural features may be shortchanged.

It's not just the hackneyed old saws of mindless replication that get in the way of good home design. When a custom-built house slavishly follows its occupants' preconceived wishes, the square pegs of preformed ideas are often forced into the round holes of site, budget, common sense, and even beauty. The only reason to hire a professional designer is to see the forest for the trees—to actually use the architect's inspired perspective.

On the other hand, if the architect writes all the rules, a house can end up being a sculpture that just happens to be occupied, dealing more with abstractions of shape, space, and light than comfort, accommodation, and usefulness. A building born solely of an architect's imagination is unlikely to delight its occupants. It's when all parties tweak each other's predilections in the design process that homes take on a life of their own.

THE WALLS OF A SCREEN PORCH don't just keep the bugs out, they can also work as art. Here, simple trim pieces are cut to botanical shapes and applied to the outside face of the framing.

Like the proverbial omelet's broken eggs, it's the unexpected positive result from banal beginnings that has the most impact. We are forced to deal with the tyranny of rules every day, and home design rules are not just mannerly and aesthetic any more. It used to be that rules like "The house must always face the street" and "Bedrooms should always be on the same floor" were all homebuilders had to respect. Increasingly, rules are being applied to building design by the government in well-intentioned efforts to protect us and our environment from ourselves.

There are millions of rules manifest in the stock plan homes that surround us, but they all follow one basic canon: They go along with the tried and true at the expense of the thoughtful to create a marketable product. The rule breakers presented in this book (otherwise known as architects and their clients) take the best that convention has to offer (economy, surety, and availability) and give those "safe" qualities life.

A CHIMNEY DOESN'T HAVE TO BE CENTERED on a façade. "Dynamic balance" can be a more effective way to organize a façade when it must respond to the home's interior and the way it sits on the land, breaking the "rule" of symmetry.

Don't Start with a Style, End with One

Frank Lloyd Wright once said that houses should have style but not a style. What he meant, of course, was not to be a slave to any particular style. But we seem to need a style when we talk about houses. Historians use them to identify significant houses, brokers use them—sometimes wrongly—to sell houses, and I've even had clients who were upset with me because I could not identify one of my house designs with a particular style. It's almost as if a label—such as colonial, contemporary, or shingle style—would make it seem real and understandable. For better or worse, these labels have stuck, but when people describe houses with style labels, what they are actually referring to are exterior characteristics—the particular blend of rooflines, siding, trim, windows, doors, and porches. It's the sum of all these parts that gives a house style, but don't necessarily give it a style.

Labels can be useful, but they are also limiting, as there is no such thing as a pure example of any one style, only a few examples from the past that seem to exemplify that style best. All other examples are only approximations. A house can also have many styles, or what I prefer to call personalities. It can look a certain way from a distance and another way up close. Its many parts such as rooflines,

NEW ENGLAND STARK but elegantly composed, this house is at once both traditional and modern.

HOUSE PARTS SHOULD "READ" and not be a slave to any style; here, the living hall in the foreground and the master bedroom wing beyond do just that.

230

ONE OF THE DEFINING characteristics of any house with style is
its roof.

materials, chimneys, colors, and trim transmit all kinds of
messages about the nature and quality of a house. Just
moving some walls, changing colors, or changing clapboards for stucco can change the personality in subtle or
dramatic ways.

If you start with a style in mind, you'll end up with it,
but often at the expense of a distinctive solution—one that
integrates site, floor plan, the exterior, and quality details
inside and out. This isn't easy. There are trade-offs everywhere you look, and you'll find yourself constantly weigh-
ing options, trying to balance function and aesthetics. The
stakes are high, because if you get it wrong the house will
always seem awkward, as so many new houses do these
days. But if you get it right, as the 50 examples in this book
illustrate, your house will most assuredly have STYLE.

EVEN A MODEST COTTAGE can have a style that is
derived from its simple, inexpensive parts.

Architects and Designers

Few undertakings are more satisfying than a successful design and building project. The secret to success lies in a clear vision and a partnership between owner and architect. If you've always wanted to have an architect design the house of your dreams, this book will help you refine your vision and focus on details that appeal to you and complement your lifestyle. It will also demonstrate the value of working with an architect.

Architects can help clients shape their ideas. They can help determine the scale that fits your lifestyle, choosing quality over quantity and responding to your needs and desires. They can also design a house that fits into its surroundings and takes advantage of the natural features of the site. All of these efforts combine to give the client a house of distinctive quality that can reflect a sense of fun and family, as shown in the homes featured in these pages

By bringing together a wide array of homes designed over the past several years, this book reminds us that good design is an investment in both the present and the future. The houses presented illustrate a range of styles and functions, from those designed to promote the use of sustainable materials and processes to updates of classic house styles. Each design is intended to enhance the quality of life for the homeowners and contribute to the vibrancy of the community.

Richard Hayes, AIA

BAUER, FREEMAN, MCDERMOTT:
ARCHITECTURE
Michael Bauer, AIA
1424 Paseo de Peralta
Santa Fe, NM 87501
(508) 988-1905
www.bfmarc.com
(pp. 112–115)

BAYLISS BRAND WAGNER ARCHITECTS
Johan Luchsinger, AIA, &
Robin Luchsinger, AIA
10801 Main St.
Bellevue, WA 98004
(425) 454-0566
www.baylissarchitects.com
(pp. 172–175)

STEPHEN BLATT ARCHITECTS
Stephen Blatt
10 Danforth St.
Portland, ME 04112
(207) 761-5911
www.sbarchitects.com
(pp. 64–67)

BLUE SKY DESIGN
4505 Roburn Rd.
Hornby Island, BC
Canada V0R1Z0
(250) 335-0115
www.blueskydesign.ca
(pp. 208–211)

BOHLIN CYWINSKI JACKSON
Peter Q. Bohlin, FAIA
8 West Market St., Suite 1200
Wilkes-Barre, PA 18701
(570) 825-8756
www.bcj.com
(pp. 80–83)

BREESE ARCHITECTS
PO Box 2726
Vineyard Haven, MA 02568
(508) 693-8272
www.breesearchitects.com
(pp. 28–31)

CENTERBROOK ARCHITECTS
AND PLANNERS
67 Main Street, PO Box 955
Centerbrook, CT 06409
(860) 767-0175
www.centerbrook.com
(pp. 52–55)

ROSS CHAPIN ARCHITECTS
Ross Chapin, AIA
PO Box 230
Langley, WA 98260
(360) 221-2373
www.rosschapin.com
(pp. 220–223)

CHENG DESIGN
Fu-Tung Cheng
2808 San Pablo Ave.
Berkeley, CA 94702
(510) 849-3272
www.chengdesign.com
(pp. 192–195)

CUTLER/ANDERSON ARCHITECTS
James Cutler, FAIA
135 Parfitt Way SW
Brainbridge Island, WA 98110
(206) 842-4710
www.cutler-anderson.com
(pp. 200–203)

HOWARD DAVIS
1836 E. 19th St.
Eugene, OR 97403
(541) 342-6247
(pp. 196–199)

DUO DICKINSON, ARCHITECT
Duo Dickinson, AIA
94 Bradley Road
Madison, CT 06443
(203) 245-0405
www.duodickinson.com
(pp. 228–229)

DRAGER GOULD ARCHITECTS
Bret Drager
625 South Commerce St., Suite 310
Tacoma, WA 98402
www.dragergould.com
(253) 593-0131
(pp. 212–215)

DUANY-PLATER-ZYBERK & CO.
Andrés Duany
1023 SW 25th Ave
Miami, FL 33135
(305) 644-1023
www.dpz.com
(pp. 100–103)

JEREMIAH ECK ARCHITECTS
Jeremiah Eck, FAIA
560 Harrison Ave., Suite 403
Boston, MA 02118
(617) 367-9696
www.jearch.com
(pp. 230–231)

ELLIOT ELLIOT NORELIUS
ARCHITECTURE
Main Street, PO Box 318
Blue Hill, ME 04614
(207) 374-2566
www.elliottelliottnorelius.com
(pp. 40–43)

ESTES/TWOMBLY ARCHITECTS
James Estes, AIA
79 Thames St.
Newport, RI 02840
(401) 846-3336
www.estestwombly.com
(pp. 72–75)

CURTIS GELOTTE ARCHITECTS
Curtis Gelotte, AIA
150 Lake Street South, Suite 208
Kirkland, WA 98033
(425) 828-3081
www.gelotte.com
(pp. 204–207)

GENESIS ARCHITECTURE
Kenneth Dahlin. AIA
4061 N. Main St., Suite 200
Rascine, WI 53402
(262) 752-1894
www.genesisarchitecture.com
(pp. 144–147)

JAMES GIVENS DESIGN
James Givens
1059 Adams Street
Eugene, OR 97402
(541) 945-5053
www.jamesgivensdesign.com
(pp. 188–191)

GROUNDSWELL ARCHITECTS
Ted Montgomery
477 Ten Stones Circle
Charlotte, VT 05445
(802) 425-7717
www.groundswellarchitects.com
(pp. 48–51)

HOUSE & HOUSE ARCHITECTS
Cathi House & Steven House, AIA
1499 Washington St.
San Francisco, CA 94109
(415) 474-2112
(pp. 108–111)

HUESTIS/TUCKER ARCHITECTS
Jennifer Huestis
2349 Whitney Ave
Hamden, CT 06518
(203) 248-1007
www.huestistucker.com
(pp. 76–79)

Architects and Designers 233

Architects and Designers

HUTKER ARCHITECTS
Phil Regan
PO Box 2347, Tisbury Market Pl.
79 Beach Rd.
Vineyard Haven, MA 02568
(508) 693-3344
www.hutkerarchitects.com
(pp. 56–59)

MICHAEL G. IMBER ARCHITECT
Michael Imber, AIA
111 West El Prado
San Antonio, TX 78212
(210) 824-7703
www.michaelgimber.com
(pp. 104–107)

GLEN IRANI ARCHITECTS
Glen Irani, AIA
410 Sherman Canal
Venice, CA 90291
(310) 305-8840
www.glenirani.com
(pp. 180–183)

HUGH NEWELL JACOBSEN, ARCHITECT
Hugh Newell Jacobsen, FAIA
2529 P. Street NW
Washington, DC 20007
(202) 337-5200
www.hughjacobsen.com
(pp. 92–95)

KNIGHT ASSOCIATES ARCHITECTS
Robert Knight, AIA
157 Hinckley Ridge
Blue Hill, ME 04614
(207) 374-2845
www.knightarchitect.com
(pp. 32–35)

LAWRENCE ARCHITECTURE
Thomas Lawrence
320 Terry Ave. North
Seattle, WA 98109
www.lawrencearchitecture.com
(206) 332-1832
(pp. 184–187)

PAUL LUKEZ ARCHITECTURE
Paul Lukez, AIA
7 Davis Square, Studio #10
Somerville, MA 02144
(617) 628-9160
www.lukez.com
(pp. 68–71)

BRIAN MACKAY-LYONS ARCHITECTURE
2188 Gottingen St.
Halifax, Nova Scotia
CANADA B3K 3B4
(902) 429-1867
www.bmlaud.ca
(pp. 44–47)

MCINTURFF ARCHITECTS
4220 Leewood Pl.
Bethesda, MD 20816
(301) 299-3705
www.mcinturffarchitects.com
(pp. 84–87)

THE MILLER/HULL PARTNERSHIP
Craig Curtis, AIA, & Sian Roberts, AIA
The Polson Building
71 Columbia—6th Floor
Seattle, WA 98104
(206) 682-6837
www.millerhull.com
(pp. 168–171)

MORGANTE-WILSON ARCHITECTS, LTD.
3813 N. Ravenswood
Chicago, IL 60613
(773) 528-1001
www.morgantewilson.com
(pp. 124–127)

NEUMANN MENDRO ANDRULAITIS
ARCHITECTS
Andy Neumann, AIA
888 Linden Ave.
Carpenteria, CA 93013
(805) 684-8885
www.nmaarchitects.com
(pp. 160–163)

FREDERICK PHILLIPS & ASSOCIATES
Frederick Phillips, FAIA
1456 N. Dayton St., Suite 200
Chicago, IL 60622
(312) 255-0415
www.frederickphillips.com
(pp. 120–123)

PRENTISS ARCHITECTS, INC.
Geoffrey Prentiss, AIA
224 West Galer
Seattle, WA 98119
(206) 283-9930
www.prentissarch.com
(pp. 164–167)

RALPH RAPSON & ASSOCIATES
Ralph Rapson, FAIA
409 Cedar Avenue South
Minneapolis, MN 55454
(612) 333-4561
www.rapsonarchitects.com
(pp. 136–139)

REHKAMP LARSON ARCHITECTS, INC.
Jean Rehkamp Larson, AIA with Steve Mooney
(project completed while at SALA Architects, Inc.)
2732 West 43rd St.
Minneapolis, MN 55410
(612) 285-7275
www.rehkamplarson.com
(pp. 116–119)

ROCKHILL & ASSOCIATES
Dan Rockhill
1546 E. 350 Rd
LeCompton, KS 66050
(785) 864-4024
www.rockhillandassociates.com
(pp. 152–155)

SALA ARCHITECTS, INC
Michaela Mahady, AIA, and Dan Porter
904 South 4th St.
Stillwater, MN 55082
(651) 351-0961
www.salaarc.com/
(pp. 148–151)

SHIM-SUTCLIFFE ARCHITECTS
Bridgette Shim, International Assoc. AIA, &
Howard Sutcliffe
441 Queen St. East
Toronto, Ontario
Canada M5A 1T5
(416) 368-3892
www.shim-sutcliffe.com
(pp. 140–143)

CASS CALDER SMITH ARCHITECTURE, INC.
44 McLea Court
San Francisco, CA 94103
(415) 864-2800
www.ccs-architecture.com
(pp. 216–219)

JAMES STERLING ARCHITECT
James Sterling, AIA
142 High Street
Portland, ME 04112
(207) 772-0037
(pp. 36–39)

STUDIO ATKINSON
Stephen Atkinson, NCARB, AIA
546 Guinda St.
Palo Alto, CA 94301
www.studioatkinson.com
(650) 321-6118
(pp. 96–99)

STUDIO B ARCHITECTS
Scott Lindenau, AIA
555 N. Mill St.
Aspen, CO 81611
(970) 920-9428
www.studiobarchitects.net
(pp. 176–179)

SUSANKA STUDIOS
Sarah Susanka, AIA
2600 Salisbury Plain
Raleigh, NC 27613
www.susanka.com
(pp. 132–135)

Architects and Designers

TURNBULL GRIFFIN HAESLOOP ARCHITECTS
Eric Haesloop, AIA
817 Bancroft Way
Berkeley, CA 94710
(510) 841-9000
www.tgharchs.com
(pp. 156–159)

VERSACI NEUMANN & PARTNERS ARCHITECTS
Russell Versaci, AIA
205 East Washington St.
Middleburg, VA 20118
(540) 687-3917
www.versacineumann.com
(pp. 88–91)

CHARLES WARREN, ARCHITECT
Charles Warren, AIA
52 West 27th St.
New York, NY 10001
(212) 625-9222
www.charleswarren.com
(pp. 60–63)

DENNIS WEDLICK ARCHITECT
Dennis Wedlick, AIA
85 Worth St., 4th floor
New York, NY 10013
(212) 625-9222
www.denniswedlick.com
(pp. 24–27)

WHEELER KEARNS ARCHITECTS
Dan Wheeler, FAIA
343 S. Dearborn St., Suite 200
Chicago, IL 60604
(312) 939-7787
www.wkarch.com
(pp. 128–131)

YESTERMORROW DESIGN/BUILD SCHOOL
John Connell, AIA
189 VT Route 100
Warren, VT 05674
(802) 496-5545
www.yestermorrow.org
(pp. 226–227)